Modern Cocktails

Dozens of Cool and Classic Mixed Drinks to Make You the Life of the Party

Modern Cocktails

Dozens of Cool and Classic Mixed Drinks to Make You the Life of the Party

Modern Cocktails

Dozens of Cool and Classic Mixed Drinks to Make You the Life of the Party

Modern Cocktails

Dozens of Cool and Classic Mixed Drinks to Make You the Life of the Party

S
P

Skyhorse Publishing

JIMMY DYMOTT // PHOTOS BY INGVAR ERIKSSON // TRANSLATED BY CORY KLINGSPORN

Mo

Cock

Dozens o

Classic Mixed

You the Lif

JIMM

Sky

JIMMY DYMOTT // PHOTOS BY INGVAR

orn

tails

Cool and

rinks to Make

f the Party

YMOTT

ng

/ TRANSLATED BY CORY KLINGSPORN

CONTENTS

Introduction No 1

—here's how it all started

I began my career as a bartender when I was nineteen, and I quickly realized I was on the right track. It was clear that I was meant to stand behind a bar, and that being a bartender would be perfect for me.

I began studying drinks and analyzing bartenders' techniques, without the slightest idea that this was the beginning of an obsession that has yet to end. Even today, I can't sit at a bar without analyzing each and every movement, each and every drink, glass, tool, type of ice, list of drinks, structure, etc., etc. . . . I love it. But at the same time, it's something of a curse—in a space where others can relax, my mind is still at work.

When I began my career behind the bar, there weren't many cocktail bars in Sweden, and the bar scene itself had reached an all-time low a few years before with the introduction of the Galliano Hot Shot—Sweden's most advanced and cherished alcoholic drink.

Its been said that Galliano opened a new factory in order to meet the demands of the Swedish market for the vanilla-flavored liqueur that was destined to be mixed with coffee and cream. I've heard horror stories from bartenders who would prepare in advance several hundred of the coffee- and Galliano-layered shots, so they could simply top them with cream as the orders came in. It's also been said that Galliano had to close the new factory just a few years later, when the Hot Shot craze died out as quickly as it had taken over. Fact or fiction, it makes for a good story.

At the time that I got started in the industry, the offerings of most bars were a catastrophe: you blended a powdered sour-mix (every bartender from those years will remember Franco's Lime and Orange mixers), juices came in jars, and cranberry juice was the hot new thing. Nobody took the profession seriously, with the exception of a select few significantly older bartenders who were already part of the "old gang" fifteen years earlier.

But things were about to change. Enthusiasts in London and New York began to add new zeal to the profession, using freshly squeezed juices and adding fresh fruit and purées to their cocktails. We'd constantly be traveling there and back for inspiration (this was before the Internet existed, so you had to actually talk to people in person and hunt them down in crowded places—ah, the good old days). There were even some who'd pack up their speed pourers and shakers and head for those places where everything was happening, so they could acquire invaluable knowledge about service, technique, and drinks.

Some of us stayed behind and did what we could to convince restaurateurs that they shouldn't see the bar as an unnecessary evil, or see bartenders as a bunch of drunks who just wanted to meet women and get wasted. And slowly but surely, things started to change back in Sweden, too. With age and experience, one had more of a say in things, and to be honest, it wasn't that difficult to stand out at the beginning when the majority of bartenders weren't willing to put in the effort that's required to run a bar with higher standards.

I was one of those who had the confidence to work in the ambitious way that I wanted. It wasn't easy, but the reward was so powerful: satisfied guests, professional pride, newspaper reviews, satisfied restaurateurs, more

Please CONTINUE

responsibility, better pay, bigger tips, and recognition from colleagues. The more you gave, the more you got back; I became completely obsessed with my work and wanted only to know more, to develop as much as I could. With these changes, completely new kinds of guests came to the bar and were interested in what was going on; the discussions and the general mood in the bar were also different. When you really care, the customers know it, and for us that opened up a whole new world. Everything was better.

Now the industry has come quite far, and with the Internet, the world has simultaneously shrunk and expanded in a way that we would never have thought possible. Any day you want, you can go online and travel the world in search of inspiration. We've also come a certain distance when it comes to taste. At the beginning, it was all about light spirits, and everything had to be masked with fruit; now we're serving stiff cocktails with strong spirits, like the Star Cocktail. People have really begun to appreciate the taste of alcohol, which makes my job so much more fun.

I've had the good fortune to be able to open more bars in Stockholm than any other bartender, and I've been involved in the development of Sweden's modern cocktail scene. It's been hard work, but at the same time, unbelievably fun. This book is something of a recap of that time, but above all, it's really a damn awesome book of drinks.

Once upon a time . . .

I thought I'd try to explain a bit about the era that inspired modern cocktail culture, since so much of the industry builds on what others have done in the past.

The cocktail and the bartending profession hail from America; its heyday ran from about 1850 to 1935. The bar was where people met before work, during work, and after work (assuming they still had work). The bar was the obvious middle ground, and the bartender was the star. Bartenders often belonged to "the Sporting Fraternity"—that is, people who lived to bet on horses and boxing matches. They were usually also well-traveled, and offered immeasurable wisdom from behind the counter. Of course, people drank themselves stupid far too often, and the harmful effects of alcohol had yet to be discovered—apart from those effects that the wives and children had to put up with when the men were drunk, so it's not difficult to understand why Prohibition was introduced.

It was during this time that bartenders like Jerry Thomas, O. H. Byron, Harry Johnson, Thomas Stuart, and Harry Craddock, to name a few, wrote their bartending manuals, which now serve as bibles for the modern bartender. Initially, these were written simply for the authors' fellow tradesmen, and were not intended to be read by other folk. Since you couldn't just walk to the nearest supermarket (or liquor store, for that matter), these men prepared everything from scratch: bitters, flavored syrups, soda, spirits, and everything else they needed. They were chemists, mixologists, psychologists, entertainers, ruffians, gamblers, and yes, heroes. These books have since been rediscovered by enthusiasts and reproduced, so that the new generation has been able to learn the principles of the trade.

A few years later, a new era of cocktails swept across the world, and bartenders have once again become a class of professionals, practicing their craft with pride. The tradition is protected, the trade taken seriously; once again, we can enjoy cocktails like Corpse Revivers, Brandy Crustas, and perfect Old Fashioneds, while also creating new drinks with the help of new techniques, new ingredients, and modern ideas. It's a wonderful time to sit in bars, try new creations, and discover new tastes.

Cocktails have never tasted—or been—better than they are now!

Bartender Talk

—everything you need to know to get started

I call my bartender philosophy "no shortcut bartending," an expression coined by the legendary Dale DeGroff. It means that I make everything from scratch. I squeeze fresh fruit juice as the drinks are ordered, make my own flavored syrups (cordials, Rock Candy), and saw and cut down blocks of ice to just the right size. I want to always be able to stand proudly behind my product and know exactly what sort of ingredients I'm working with. So when I say mint, lemon, lime, orange, or any other fruit, herb, or spice, I mean it should be fresh and of the best quality.

In the recipes that follow, there are a few key terms and expressions, so here are some explanations to help you keep things straight.

ORANGE PEEL is the outer peel of an orange, which I cut off the fruit. Then, I press the oils out of it and into the drink. The same goes for lemon peel and grapefruit peel, with their respective fruits.

To **MUDDLE** is to crush sugar and herbs or fruit in the bottom of a mixing glass or shaker with a so-called muddler.

MARASCHINO CHERRIES are Marasca cherries in syrup that are used to garnish and, occasionally, flavor; not to be confused with Maraschino liqueur.

DRY-SHAKE means to shake mixtures containing egg whites in a shaker without ice, to work the egg whites into a foam.

To **COAT** a glass means to spray the inside of it with spirits or bitters in order to subtly flavor the drink, so that the liquor is blended and altered within the glass.

A **BAR SPOON** is (in addition to being a tool) a measurement of one teaspoon.

TOOLS

As a bartender, I use a wide range of tools to mix drinks. You don't need quite as many at home, but in order to be able to mix really good, attractive drinks, you'll be much better off with a set of basic tools. The most important are:

JIGGER (A KIND OF MEASURING GLASS)
BAR SPOON
MUDDLER
MIXING GLASS
SHAKER
KNIFE
STRAINER (COCKTAIL SIEVE)
ICE TONGS

For a more thorough description of these tools and others, see Tools and Glasses on page 72.

Syrups, Cordials, and Juice

Throughout this book, I use a variety of syrups and cordials—a syrup made with fruit juice and, occasionally, fruit peels. There are, of course, cordials and flavored syrups available for purchase, but the process is more fun and the results taste better when it's homemade.

The following are some basic recipes for the cordials, syrups, and other mixers that show up in the book.

SIMPLE SYRUP
1 part water
1 part granulated sugar

Boil the water; mix in the sugar. Stir until the sugar is completely dissolved. Let cool, and pour into a glass bottle. Keeps for up to two months in the fridge.

ORANGE CORDIAL
10 fl oz (300 ml) freshly-squeezed
*   orange juice*
orange peels
1 1/4 cup (300 ml) granulated sugar
1/3 fl oz (10 ml) vodka

Press oranges until you have 10 fl oz of juice; pour this into a saucepan. Cut the peel off of the pressed oranges and place these in the saucepan as well. Add the sugar, boil the mixture, and let it simmer for a few minutes. Remove the peels and reduce to the desired consistency. Allow to cool. Pour into a glass bottle. Combine with about 1/3 oz (10 ml) or so of vodka and it'll keep in the fridge for a couple of weeks without any problems.

LIME CORDIAL
10 fl oz (300 ml) freshly squeezed
*   lime juice*
lime peels
1 1/4 cup (300 ml) granulated sugar
1/3 oz (10 ml) vodka

Squeeze the limes until you have 10 fl oz of lime juice; pour this into a saucepan. Cut the peel off of the pressed limes and place these in the saucepan as well. Add the sugar, boil the mixture, and let it simmer for a few minutes. Remove the peels and reduce to the desired consistency. I usually add a bit more sugar rather than risk reducing the mixture too much. Allow to cool. Pour into a glass bottle.

Combine with about 1/3 oz (10 ml) or so of vodka and it'll keep in the fridge for a couple of weeks without any problems.

GRENADINE
1 part granulated sugar
1 part pomegranate juice
(orange flower water, optional)
1/3 fl oz (10 ml) vodka

Mix the sugar and pomegranate juice until the sugar is dissolved. I also like to add a few drops of orange flower water. No heating is needed; just pour this into a glass bottle with about 1/3 oz (10 ml) of vodka and it'll keep in the fridge for up to a month.

RASPBERRY SYRUP
10 fl oz (300 ml) granulated sugar
1 1/4 cup (300 ml) raspberries
   (I use frozen ones)
10 fl oz (300 ml) water
1/3 fl oz (10 ml) vodka

Mix sugar and raspberries in a bowl.
Boil water and pour over the mixture;
refrigerate for two hours. Strain and
pour into a glass bottle. With 1 1/3
oz (10 ml) of vodka, it'll keep in the
fridge for a couple of weeks without
problems.

PASSION FRUIT SYRUP
2 passion fruits
1 1/4 cup (300 ml) granulated sugar
10 fl oz (300 ml ml) water
1 1/3 oz (10 ml) vodka

Cut open and hollow out the passion
fruits. Mix the passion fruit seeds with
the sugar. Boil water; pour over the
mixture and refrigerate for two hours.
Strain and pour into a glass bottle. With
1 1/3 oz (10 ml) of vodka, it'll keep in
the fridge for a couple of weeks without
problems.

ROCK CANDY SYRUP
2 1/2 cups (600 ml) granulated sugar
1 qt (1 L) water

Heat an aluminum saucepan and distribute
the sugar in it. Stir periodically until
the sugar begins to clump and turn light
brown.
   When all the sugar has melted and
become liquid, add the water. Pour in
a bit of the water at a time, stirring
constantly until all of the water is
completely mixed in. Reduce for about
10-15 minutes and allow to cool. Pour
into a jar that has been cleaned with
boiling water. This can be stored at room
temperature for almost any length of
time.

HONEY WATER
2 parts water
1 part honey

Boil water; stir in honey (I use acacia
honey). Allow to cool and pour into a
glass bottle. Keeps for up to one month
in the fridge.

THE BASICS

A good liquor cabinet doesn't need to be packed. You just need a selection of basic spirits (see *Spirits* on page 113), and a few other alcoholic drinks. I ought to say that in addition to the basics, if you keep the following at home, you'll be able to make quite a few different cocktails:

RED VERMOUTH
DRY VERMOUTH
MARASCHINO LIQUEUR
COINTREAU
ANGOSTURA BITTERS
ORANGE BITTERS

If you want to expand your range even further, I'd add some herbal liqueurs or Campari.

Juleps

The history of the julep goes quite a long way back. References to eighth-century Persia feature people drinking jallab, a drink made of a grape, rose petal, and fig syrup that was mixed with crushed ice, water, raisins, and pine nuts—though it was initially made with just sugar, water, and rose petals. Until the 1600s, the julep was most commonly a non-alcoholic drink, and it was consumed strictly for medicinal purposes.

During the early 1800s, mint found its way into the julep. In 1804, it was mentioned in an American newspaper article under the name Mint Sling, and a few years later, the addition of mint had become standard, along with the name julep. The julep and the cobbler were drinks made with ice, and until the end of the decade, they were the preferred drinks for those in the know.

Today, when we speak of the Mint Julep we think of the South, the Kentucky Derby, and above all, bourbon. But it began with brandy, though there are even some who claim that a true julep only uses rye whiskey. There are also those who insist that the julep should only contain spearmint—no other kind of mint is acceptable—and that the drink must be served wrapped in a napkin to keep it from being warmed unnecessarily. As with all classics, there are too many "dos and don'ts" associated with the drink to count them all.

In 1938, it was decided at the Churchill Downs racetrack, where the Kentucky Derby is held, that Early Times bourbon and the Mint Julep would be the race's official drinks. Every year, more than 120,000 Juleps are mixed in a single weekend! I don't know how many I've mixed myself, but I thought I'd give you the recipe for a Mint Julep, and some suggestions for tried-and-true variants.

MINT JULEP
2 1/2 fl oz (70 ml) bourbon
a handful of mint leaves
1 cup (250 ml) simple syrup
crushed ice
10 sprigs of mint for garnish

Place the mint in a julep cup (or a glass of similar size), and pour in the syrup and bourbon. Fill half the cup with crushed ice, and stir with a bar spoon until the outside of the cup is cold. Top with more crushed ice and stir again. Garnish with mint sprigs around the rim of the entire cup—the idea is to bury your nose in the leaves when drinking, to increase the mint flavor. As an alternative to bourbon, you can also try rye whiskey, which has more of a peppery taste, but even brandy, gin, or rum will work quite well in a julep. You can make a Prescription Julep by mixing equal parts rye whiskey and brandy.

Jerry Thomas made a variant known as the Georgia Mint Julep with equal parts brandy and peach brandy. Peach brandy isn't exactly the easiest thing to get a hold of, but I made a variant using apricot brandy that was also quite good, and there are even peach bitters, if you'd like to go that route.

...VER SATIN - GIN, L...

...ONZE COCKTAIL - GIN,

...LIOT LAUNCESTON SOUR -

...LE ANGELF**K - VODI...

...DNIGHT SHIFTER - TEC...

...OM RUM TO WHISKEY - RU...

...RD & 3RD - J.D. 1 BARRE...

...OOKED COCKTAIL - BO...

...BITTERED COLLINS - B...

...LO #2 - RUM, LIME,

a bartender's résumé

First of all, you've got to know what kind of bar you want to run. Then, you've got to consider what's possible, logistically and financially speaking, and what you've got the skills for. Everything depends on your team, and you're never stronger than the weakest link. But let's say you've got all this under control, and you've decided to make yourself a menu of, say, twenty drinks, there is still quite a lot to take into consideration.

Every menu's got to have a couple of big ticket items—drinks you know bar patrons are going to go ape for and that are going to sell like hotcakes. Usually these are simple flavor combinations that you know will hit home. Then, you want to have some proper showpieces, where you can flex your muscles and show who's boss: advanced, visually striking drinks.

Then you've got to consider the range of available liquors, and here, the bar's profile plays a big part—which country, style, or movement is your influence. Every bar ought to have a small list of classics, to show that you've got a good grip on the basics, and even here you can show people what kind of bar you run. In addition, you should always have a couple of drinks where you compromise on alcohol content (but not on taste)—so-called low-alcohol cocktails, based on apéritifs, vermouths, and herbal liqueurs.

You've also got to have a range of different categories of drinks, such as sours, fizzes, cobblers, flips, and champagne cocktails, to name a few (I'll go through these later in the book).

Once you've tackled all of these questions, you can start to approach a concept and an idea of what you want to do; then you can take a look at your team and discuss what you can manage under pressure. There's nothing worse than a bar with a menu that it can't deliver on a crowded night; patrons shouldn't have to wait too long, and there should never be any problem preparing a drink

you put on the menu. When you've done all of that and learned how to prep for the menu you've made, no drink should take longer than two to three minutes to make. The key to success is in the prep work—i.e., those preparations you make before serving drinks—but also in the way you work: cleanliness, cleaning up after yourself, and making sure that everything gets put back where it belongs, so that your colleagues don't have to stop and think when they reach their work station and are about to mix a drink.

Once these fundamentals are well established, I'd say you ought to change your drink list at least twice a year. Always try to follow the seasons, assuming you don't have some sort of bar concept that goes completely against this. At the bars I currently run, Marie Laveau and Little Quarter, we change the drink list once a month, and we create every drink ourselves. At Little Quarter, we started off by changing the menu every other week, and we exclusively mixed classics, but we quickly got tired of it and started serving only our own drinks inspired by classics—so-called contemporary classics. We've also had a long drink menu where flavored cordials and syrups laid the foundations for fizzes, long drinks, and cobblers, all based on the fruits that were in season.

This notion can, of course, be adjusted for the home bar, whenever you're thinking about offering cocktails. It's easy to get the impression that it takes a fully stocked liquor cabinet to mix good cocktails, but you can actually go quite a long way even with limited means. Start with a couple of spirits you are partial to, and learn some drinks with these as bases. At least make a set of syrups to keep in your fridge, and you'll be well on your way. Then, all you really need is fresh fruit, herbs, and spices in order to make enough drinks for a successful cocktail party.

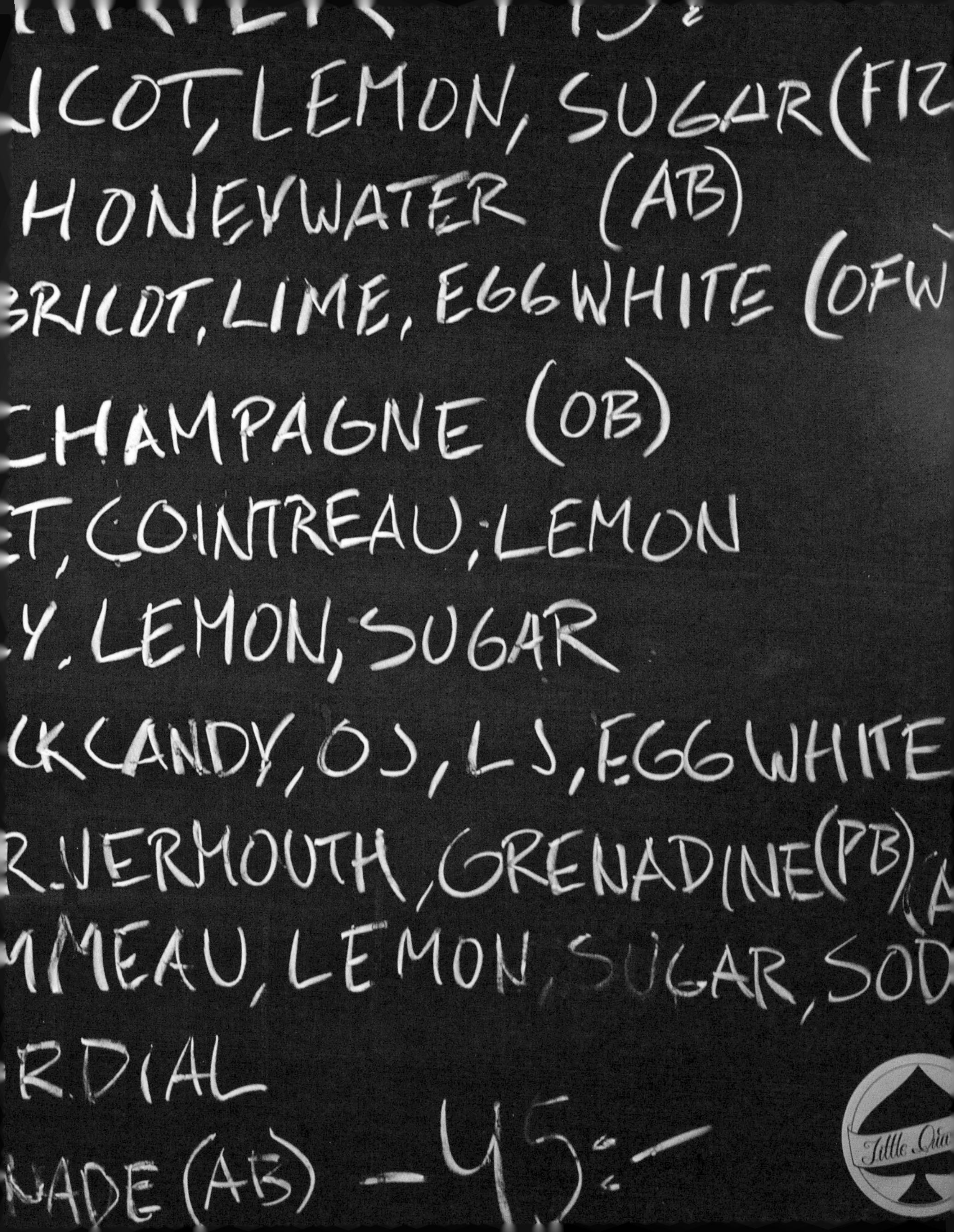

ICOT, LEMON, SUGAR (FIZ

HONEYWATER (AB)

BRICOT, LIME, EGGWHITE (OFW

CHAMPAGNE (OB)

T, COINTREAU, LEMON

Y, LEMON, SUGAR

CK CANDY, OJ, LJ, EGGWHITE

R.VERMOUTH, GRENADINE (PB)

MMEAU, LEMON, SUGAR, SOD

R.DIAL

NADE (AB) — U5) —

Mardi Gras

When we opened Marie Laveau in 2005, Daniel Olsson and I made a drink list with a few more classics and some stiffer versions of cocktails. I'd become more and more interested in classic cocktails and mixing drinks with brown spirits, which felt like a bit more of a challenge.

One drink we made, which is still on the list today, and is still a best-seller, is the Mardi Gras. We used a new kind of bitter we'd gotten our hands on: Peychaud's Bitters—a classic New Orleans bitter that's strongly associated with the origin of the word "cocktails." For a long time, it was claimed that the creator, Antoine Amedie Peychaud, had served it in small egg cups in his store (or apothecary, as it were) in New Orleans. To get people to drink this concoction, which was supposed to be good for various ailments, he mixed it with cognac and later with rye whiskey and a bit of sugar—quite like the basic recipe for a cocktail made with strong spirits, sugar, bitters, and water.

From the beginning, cocktails were served more as "tonics"—that is, small doses that were mixed with water and ice, and they were considered to be medicines to be knocked back. The story goes that the drink served in egg cups, called *coquetier* in French, later evolved into "cocktail" in America. It's since been established that the name didn't come about this way at all, and that literary references to the word were found to exist in poetry and newspapers much earlier than this, but I've always liked the story and I'm convinced that Peychaud has played a large part in the history and popularity of the cocktail.

2 1/3 fl oz (70 ml) bourbon
1 fl oz (30 ml) honey
1 1/3 fl oz (40 ml)
   freshly squeezed lemon juice
3-4 splashes Peychaud's Bitters

There's a little trick you'll need to know in order to get the Mardi Gras to blend properly. First, pour the honey into the shaker, and then pour the bourbon on top. After that, loosen up the honey with the back of a bar spoon, or else it'll solidify in the shaker and the drink won't have the proper sweetness. Next, add the lemon juice and Peychaud's Bitters; shake with ice and serve in a cocktail glass.

PEYCHAUD'S BITTERS CAN BE DIFFICULT TO GET A HOLD OF. IF YOU CAN'T FIND THEM USE A COMBINATION OF ANGOSTURA BITTERS AND ORANGE BITTERS INSTEAD.

Sazerac

Peychaud's cocktail, which consisted of cognac, bitters, sugar, and a drop of water, quickly gained popularity and was served in many places. A man by the name of Sewell Taylor ran a bar in New Orleans and he became the general agent for the French cognac Sazerac de Forge et Fils. When the bar changed owners, it was quickly renamed Sazerac, and people soon began calling their variant of the cocktail by the same name. Today, the drink is the official cocktail of the city of New Orleans and has been for a couple years.

Sazerac was initially mixed using cognac, but when the phylloxera plague saw the destruction of the greater part of Europe's vineyards in 1867, it was practically impossible to find cognac, so in the United States, people switched to drinking domestic spirits like rye whiskey and bourbon. I like the variant with rye whiskey the best, and it's what I serve unless I'm specifically asked to mix the drink differently.

2 1/3 fl oz (70 ml) rye whiskey
1 tsp (5 ml) absinthe
1 lump of raw sugar
2/3 fl oz (20 ml) water
4 splashes Peychaud's Bitters (or a combination
   of Angostura bitters and orange bitters)

First coat the glass with absinthe, so the interior of the glass is flavored by the absinthe. You can do this several different ways; I use a spray bottle of the same type as a perfume bottle. You can also fill the glass with crushed ice, pour in a bit of absinthe, top it off with soda water, and then dump everything out, and boom, you've got absinthe along the entire glass.

Next, soak the sugar in Peychaud's Bitters and dissolve it in a mixing glass with 2/3 fl oz (20 ml) water. Pour in the rye whiskey and add ice; stir until the sugar is completely dissolved. Pour the drink into the absinthe-coated glass and garnish with a bit of lemon peel.

This drink should be served without ice in the glass. The more the drink is warmed while being consumed, the more the absinthe and rye whiskey will mix, and the character of the drink will change gradually.

Juicy Fruit

When our restaurant Grill opened in Stockholm in 2003, we needed something special. My colleagues and I made a drink list that really stretched the limits of our know-how and put our skills to the test. One drink that soon proved to be a best-seller was the Juicy Fruit.

Drinks can come about in many ways, and you can find inspiration just about anywhere. When it comes to the Juicy Fruit, it started with a song by Mtume that was played at the Lydmar Hotel bar every single evening I worked there, for several years. The song, of course, is called Juicy Fruit, and when I stopped to think about the name, I realized it was the best name for a drink I'd ever heard. I also drew inspiration from the chewing gum, hence the mint in the drink.

The Juicy Fruit has made Stockholm's bartenders swear many a time. It's one of those drinks that you make once and then have to keep making for the rest of the night. At this time it was still a little strange to see a bartender doing high-end work, but when we opened Grill, we decided that our bar should be the best that was ever opened, and we wanted to prove just how sharp we were at our craft. The bar ended up being quite successful, and we mixed who knows how many Juicy Fruits. It was crazy.

1 fl oz (30 ml) vanilla vodka
2/3 fl oz (20 ml) Butterscotch Schnapps
1/2 passion fruit
1/2 lemon, cut into cubes
a small handful of mint leaves
2/3 fl oz (20 ml) passion fruit syrup
   (see page 13)

This drink is mixed in two stages. Start by muddling the passion fruit, lemon, and mint in an Old Fashioned glass. Add a little bit of crushed ice to keep this mixture in place, and then add the passion fruit syrup and vanilla vodka. Top off the mixture with a neat mountain of crushed ice and Butterscotch Schnapps. Finally, garnish with a sprig of mint.

Raspberry Fudge

For the opening of the restaurant Ljunggren in the Stockholm neighborhood Götgatsbacken, we put together a brand-new menu with a few real "jump-up-and-down" surprises. Drinks with names like Raspberry Fudge, Yo' Mama, Barry White, and Marrakesh stood alongside classics like the Southside, Manhattan, Hemingway Daiquiri, and the ever-present Old Fashioned.

People thought that "Ljungan"—Mikael Ljunggren himself—was crazy for opening a bar in the Söder district. Nevertheless, we decided to serve beer in 11 fl oz glasses, despite charging for a pint. We had a guy at the door whose job it was to basically deny entry to anyone he didn't know personally. Quite daring, but Ljungan's plan was for us to cater to the niche crowd of modern, hip Söder, and he dared to let us go through with it. This was at the time when people thought someone must be crazy to even dream of selling cocktails in Söder; unlike today, where there are quite a range of good cocktail bars.

Ljunggren was really fun to work with, and I got the chance to grow in more ways than just standing behind the bar. I was responsible for seeing to it that the bar had a clear-cut profile with cocktails and music, and that the staff did everything we could to sell drinks to a public that most people believed would only drink beer.

The Raspberry Fudge came about when one of my regulars got tired of drinking Juicy Fruits every day and wanted to have the same drink but something different . . . We also served this drink at Marie Laveau, but there, we served it in a tall class with crushed ice.

1 fl oz (30 ml) vanilla vodka
2/3 fl oz (20 ml) Butterscotch Schnapps
1 fl oz (30 ml) freshly squeezed lemon juice
2/3 fl oz (20 ml) simple syrup
1 1/3 fl oz (40 ml) raspberry purée
   (raspberry mixed with a bit of granulated sugar)

Combine the ingredients in a shaker with ice; shake.
Serve in a cocktail glass.

THIS IS A REAL "CANDY-DRINK" OF SORTS—ONE
THAT SPEAKS TO EVERYONE WHO LIKES A BIT OF SWEETNESS.
I SEEM TO THINK IT REMINDS ME OF A POPSICLE I HAD ONCE WHEN
I WAS LITTLE, BUT I CAN'T REMEMBER WHAT THE NAME OF IT WAS.

For the restaurant Indigo, which Robban Sörman and I opened in 2001 in the Stockholm neighborhood Götgatsbacken, we created quite a few new drinks. One that made it on to several other drink lists was the John Holmes. The drink was a tribute to the legend of the same name, and with drinks, as with so many other things, a good name sells itself. It got to be called "John" because, if someone keeps company with Jack Daniels as much as we did, you call that person John.

1 fl oz (30 ml) Jack Daniels
2/3 fl oz (20 ml) freshly squeezed lemon juice
2/3 fl oz (20 ml) simple syrup
1 fl oz (30 ml) cranberry juice
2/3 fl oz (20 ml) raspberry liquor

Build this drink by mixing all the ingredients in a tall glass with crushed ice; garnish with a blackberry (at one point, just about everything was garnished with blackberries, because the blackberry is one of the few frozen berries that doesn't lose its shape when thawed).

IF YOU DON'T KNOW
WHO JOHN HOLMES
WAS, I SUGGEST
GOOGLING HIM. AND
AS A COMMENT ON
THAT, I CAN ONLY
ADD THAT FOR ME
THE DRINK STILL
FEELS LIKE HIM:
A TAD OUTDATED
. . . BUT IF YOU
LIKE THIS SORT OF
DRINK, IT'S STILL
GOOD.

No Shortcuts
–it's all about the ingredients

At my bar Little Quarter, we've always been proud of our ability to mix classic cocktails in an atmosphere that more closely resembles a nightclub bar. My associates and I are of the opinion that a good drink takes a little bit of time to make, but if you're unsure of your flavors, it can take too much time—something a customer shouldn't have to put up with. It's important that you're able to manage your drink list, and you must be prepared to actually make the cocktails you claim to know. It's extremely irritating to see so-called mixologists who think it's acceptable to spend ten minutes mixing a drink.

Just like a good cook that delivers fantastic food, the greatest amount of work lies in the prep, or those preparations you do before the bar opens and the customers arrive. This is the greatest difference between a good bar and a merely okay one. After that, you've got to judge a bar by what it's trying to convey—not all bars are cocktail bars.

When it comes to fruit juices, there are absolutely no shortcuts; the only thing worth working with is freshly squeezed juice. I would even go so far as to say that it should be squeezed no sooner than when the customer orders the drink. But some bars are all about getting drinks out as quickly as possible, and so in that situation it's acceptable to work with juice that's been pre-squeezed.

If you're mixing drinks at home, you're definitely going to want to squeeze the juice yourself, and it will make all the difference. Try something as simple as a Screwdriver with freshly-squeezed orange juice and you'll see what I mean. If you always use good ingredients, you're guaranteed to succeed in mixing great drinks; but if you cheat, the result will always be the worse for it. Laziness is not acceptable in a bartender, and one who can't manage to put in the required amount of effort should—in my opinion—pay a visit to one who can. There are many good, proud bartenders who are ready to put in that effort every day.

Dry Martini-variants No5

FORD, P. 36

THE HEARST, P. 36

VESPER, P. 38

The following are a few classic variants for those who like a Dry Martini but want to experience something new (or old, depending on how you look at it). When it comes to the proportions in these drinks, I think it's open to interpretation and depends on how much you like vermouth and how "wet" you want your cocktail. The more vermouth you use, the wetter it'll be. I like strong spirits, and this tends to show up in the proportions I use. Experiment to find the proportions that taste best to you.

MARTINEZ, P. 37

MARGUERITE
COCKTAIL, P. 37

Ford

A personal favorite that can be found in George Kappeler's 1895 *Modern American Drinks*. The drink didn't get its name from the well-known car manufacturer, nor from Henry Ford himself; rather, it's said to come from a famed journalist and athlete named Malcolm Webster Ford, who showed up sometime in the early 1900s. It appears that after a series of financial setbacks, he took his own life. But the drink lives on and that's something, at least.

1 2/3 fl oz (50 ml) gin
2/3 fl oz (20 ml) dry vermouth
1/3 fl oz (10 ml) Bénédictine D.O.M.
4 splashes Orange Bitters

Combine the ingredients in a mixing glass with ice; stir. Pour into a martini glass and finish off the drink with a touch of orange peel; you press out the oil and leave in the glass.

The Hearst

This drink comes from *The Old Waldorf-Astoria Bar Book* (1935), written by Albert Stevens Crockett. This is a veritable bible when it comes to cocktail classics that were popular before Prohibition. It's said that a few journalists who worked for William Randolph Hearst (newspaper publisher, politician, and inspiration for *Citizen Kane,* among other things) invented the drink. They'd often drop in at the Waldorf-Astoria to have a few drinks while they were out working. Sitting in a bar and drinking cocktails in the daytime is really damn romantic from a bartender's perspective, but oh so dangerous.

1 2/3 fl oz (50 ml) gin
2/3 fl oz (20 ml) sweet vermouth
3 splashes Angostura Bitters
3 splashes Orange Bitters

Combine the ingredients in a mixing glass with ice; stir. Pour into a martini glass and top it off with a touch of orange peel; press out the oil and leave in the glass.

Martinez

It's said that this is the drink that evolved into the Dry Martini. Some claim that the sweet vermouth was substituted for dry, and the Maraschino disappeared somewhere along the way, which may or may not be true. The original was made with Old Tom Gin, a sweeter variant of gin. The drink can be found in O. H. Byron's *Modern Bartender's Guide* (1884).

1 2/3 fl oz (50 ml) gin
2/3 fl oz (20 ml) sweet vermouth
2 bar spoons of Maraschino liquor
3 splashes Angostura Bitters

Combine the ingredients in a mixing glass with ice; stir. Pour into a martini glass and garnish with a bit of orange peel and a Maraschino cherry.

Marguerite Cocktail

This drink is also linked to the Dry Martini, and the version I prefer comes from *Stuart's Fancy Drinks and How To Mix Them* by Thomas Stuart (1896).

1 2/3 fl oz (50 ml) Plymouth gin
2/3 fl oz (20 ml) dry vermouth
3 splashes Orange Bitters

Combine the ingredients in a mixing glass with ice; stir. Pour into a martini glass and top off with a touch of orange peel; press out the oil and leave in the glass.

Vesper

The Bond drink in Casino Royale was invented by Ian Fleming's buddy Ivar Bryce. To recreate it the way it was in the beginning, when Lillet was called Kina Lillet, you can add in a pinch of quinine powder. You could also look for Cocchi Americano, which contains more quinine. Personally, I'm against shaking "clear" drinks—too much air gets into the drink and it dilutes unnecessarily. But when it comes to the Bond drink, it's certainly hard not to hear "shaken, not stirred" playing in the back of your mind.

3 parts Gordon's gin
1 part vodka (Bond prefers Russian vodka)
1/2 part Lillet

Combine the ingredients in a mixing glass with ice; stir. Pour into a martini glass and finish off the drink with a touch of orange peel; press out the oil and leave in the glass.

You are a guest; behave as such

·

Respect other members' right to privacy

·

A gentleman speaks to a lady only
when she has first spoken to him

·

Smoking is to occur only in designated places

·

Use of mobile phones is to be kept to a minimum

·

When one's visit is over, the "Bakery" is to be left
in a calm, dignified way, with a taxi waiting

·

Photography is forbidden

·

Drink and relax

HOUSE RULES

Speakeasies
–from holes in the wall to hot spots

In 2008, I was contacted by Jon Lacotte, an old colleague who had started working at the Michelin Bar in the restaurant Frantzén/Lindeberg, in Stockholm's Old Town. He asked me if I'd be interested in opening up a members-only, speakeasy bar nearby that they had procured some time before. I simply couldn't refuse. I left my job and started planning a proper speakeasy-style bar with burning zeal. Speakeasies were the name for the holes in the wall that illegally served alcohol during the years of Prohibition. The name most likely comes from the fact that you had to order your drink from the bartender quietly, in a low voice—that is, you had to "speak easy." Sweden's speakeasy trend (if you can call it that) was relatively new, and for some time I had wanted to open a bar with strictly classic cocktails where I could work with the best ingredients I could get my hands on. The place was sparsely decorated, with a focus on lighting and on getting as many seats as we could to fill the relatively small space.

I made a list of strictly classic cocktails from the pre-Prohibition and Prohibition eras; that is, from about 1850 to 1933. Prohibition stretched from 1920 to 1933 and during this period, all manufacture, sale, and transport of alcohol was forbidden. Drinking itself was not illegal, and many people had their doctors prescribe alcohol for "medicinal" purposes. Prohibition caused many American bartenders to move to Europe and continue their work abroad, which meant that the American cocktail culture spread throughout the world.

In recent years, there have been a number of movies and TV series based on the time period, which has, of course, contributed to the excitement and glamour associated with it. It was, after all, during this period that the United States was molded by gangsters,

Please Continue 4

and people partied like never before—a very special time full of diverse and colorful personalities. Obviously, Hollywood has helped to boost interest in the era, though I might say that it didn't do much for cocktail-drinking itself, something that all of the world's very competent bartenders can attest to.

At f/l Cocktail Bar—or the Bakery, as my speakeasy came to be called, since the place was once a real bakery—I'd mix drinks with larger measurements, so that a cocktail would be roughly 3 fluid ounces, and I used quality spirits (which was probably the only thing that was anachronistic, given that Prohibition-era alcohol usually wasn't of the best quality). We made a member list based on my network of contacts derived from earlier loyal customers and friends. Björn and Daniel also helped with contacts from Frantzén/Lindeberg. We started small, but every member got to recommend one additional member, so things grew quickly, and after the first day I was forced to bring in some help. Vito Grip became my apprentice and the best cocktail waiter in town. He was also the bouncer, the doorman, and the dishwasher. You had to check in when you arrived, and you were only allowed to take in one guest at a time. The membership card ended up working like a sort of pass, and there were strict rules that all members were required to follow. It was one of the best bars I've ever managed, and it was always incredibly enjoyable to head off to work. The mood was always special.

After the first year, we'd grown so much that we expanded the place and made a bar within the kitchen, and we brought in two more bartenders, Joel Söderbäck and Andreas Bergman. We made almost exclusively cocktails, always of the best quality. People really appreciated the opportunity to sit in a quiet environment and enjoy perfectly-mixed drinks. Certain evenings were just magical, and it felt like we never wanted to close at the end of the night. We ran the Bakery for one more year, but unfortunately, we were forced to close it the next.

The Bakery was a tremendous effort from myself and everyone else involved. It was hard work, but it was also unbelievably positive. We were recognized internationally by Jim Meehan (the owner of what may be the world's most well-known speakeasy, Please Don't Tell or PDT), and *Esquire's* top one hundred bars ranking. We also ended up on the list of the five most interesting bars and a bar to keep one's eye on, which might not mean that much in the grand scheme of things, but it was the first time, as far as I know, that a Swedish bar got that kind of attention. Many of my personal heroes of the industry stopped in, but I've already named Jim, and that's enough name dropping. One of the rules at f/l Cocktail Bar was that you weren't allowed to discuss what went on there, nor to speak about who was a guest or a member—a rule that I continue to honor.

Those who joined us during this short time got to be a part of something incredibly special, and even today, I have customers whose eyes glaze over when somebody speaks of the Bakery and what the place meant to them. I know that we shaped and developed the Stockholmers' outlook on drinks during that short time, and many of them opened their eyes to classic cocktails and the way a good drink should taste and look. The Bakery was also what led me to open Little Quarter, which, if you ask me, is the best bar in Sweden.

Classics

A look through one of the classic bartender manuals (see my tips for legitimate, good books on page 143) might give you the impression that there are untold numbers of classic drinks. But for a drink to become a classic, it's got to maintain some sort of popularity over the years, and as with everything, there is fashion even in cocktails—what spirits you mix and which flavorings you use. Here, I've selected a crew of truly good classics.

45

Old Fashioned

For me, everything started with the Old Fashioned; the first time I drank one, I wanted to master it, and the first time I mixed one, I was hooked. When I later came to know that it's one of the world's oldest cocktails and that it's composed of only four ingredients (liquor, sugar, bitters, and water), I was completely sold. After that, I wanted to learn everything about different kinds of drinks and where they came from. The Old Fashioned is said to have been invented around 1880 by a bartender at The Pendennis Club for gentlemen in Louisville, Kentucky.

"The Old Fashioned Way" refers to mixing any kind of liquor with sugar, bitters, and water. Try, for example, an Old Fashioned with gin. Quite good. For me, it's also a good way to see what sort of skills a bartender has; if he knows his Old Fashioned, you can maybe continue down the list and set a bit more faith in him.

At any rate, for this drink you'll need the following:

2 1/3 fl oz (70 ml) bourbon or rye whiskey
1 cube of raw sugar
5 splashes of Angostura Bitters
3 pieces of orange peel
1 Maraschino cherry

Soak the sugar cube with Angostura Bitters. A cool trick is to place the sugar cube on a cloth napkin over the mixing glass and soak it in bitters, then let the liquid drip into the mixing glass. Apart from not blackening your fingers with the Angostura (which can happen when you're making 20-30 of these in an evening), the sugar will be evenly saturated and you'll be able to better control the amount of bitters that end up in the drink, in a neat way.

Dissolve the sugar in a bit of water, so that you make a quick syrup with sugar and bitters. Then, add the bourbon or rye whiskey and press in the oils from two pieces of orange peel.

Stir the mixture with ice, and pour it into a large whiskey glass. Add ice and press the oil out of the last piece of orange peel over the drink; garnish with orange peel and maraschino cherries. If you ask me, it doesn't get much better than this.

PERFECTION AND THE NECTAR OF THE GODS!

French 75

The French 75-millimeter field gun is recognized as the first modern piece of artillery—easy to move around and with a really mean kick. The gun was the favorite weapon of the French during World War I, and was also used briefly by the American expeditionary forces that were sent to back up the French and allied British in the fight against the German forces.

As the story goes, the Yanks began mixing champagne with lemon, sugar, and gin to give it a bit more of a kick, and it seems that mixing drinks was already common with them at that time (no Frenchman had ever thought to mix anything with champagne, that much is sure). One way or another, they gave this mixture the name French 75, in recognition of how bombed you'd get after knocking a couple back.

The drink made an impact in the New York Bar in Paris, later Harry's New York Bar, as well as at the Stork Club in New York. It was also a favorite at my bar, the Bakery.

1 fl oz (35 ml) gin
2/3 fl oz (20 ml) freshly squeezed
   lemon juice
2/3 fl oz (20 ml) simple syrup
champagne

Combine the gin, lemon, and syrup in a shaker. Shake well with ice and serve with ice in a tall glass. Fill the glass with ice-cold champagne.

The Bee's Knees

Another simple, but oh-so-good classic is the Bee's Knees, slang for "the height of excellence"— in other words, when something was really damn good. The Bee's Knees is a sour drink, and many of the most beloved drinks usually contain lemon or lime.

2 1/3 fl oz (70 ml) gin
1 fl oz (30 ml) honey
1 1/4 fl oz (40 ml) freshly
  squeezed lemon juice

Dissolve the honey with gin in a shaker. Add the lemon juice and shake well with ice. Serve in a cocktail glass with a bit of orange peel.

Brandy Crusta

Nowadays, mixing citrus fruits with spirits is an obvious thing to do, but that hasn't always been the case. Everything started with the Brandy Crusta, invented in 1852 by Joseph Santina, who worked at The Jewel of the South in New Orleans. The Brandy Crusta is a spicier predecessor of the Sidecar, with a bit more "oomph" to it. And note the amount of lemon—it's not a proper sour yet, but here's the foundation.

1 2/3 fl oz (50 ml) brandy or cognac
2/3 fl oz (20 ml) Cointreau
1/2 fl oz (15 ml) freshly-squeezed lemon juice
1 tsp (5 ml) Maraschino liquor
3 splashes Peychaud's Bitters

Combine the ingredients in a shaker with ice; shake. Serve the drink in a small wine glass with a sugared rim, and garnish with a large piece of lemon peel.

Sidecar

This is a true Prohibition-era classic, and perhaps
one of few drinks that was actually created during
the period. The drink supposedly gets its name from
a captain who was shuttled to and from Paris's Hotel
Ritz in a motorcycle sidecar.

1 2/3 fl oz (50 ml) brandy; alternatively, a younger cognac
1 fl oz (30 ml) Cointreau
1 fl oz (30 ml) fresh lemon juice

Combine the ingredients in a shaker with ice;
shake well. Serve in a cocktail glass with a
sugared rim, and garnish with a large piece of
lemon peel.

Margarita

The margarita is related to the Brandy Crusta and has been attributed to Margarita Sames, a bar owner from Acapulco. Others say that it was Danny Herrera, a bartender from Tijuana, who created the drink for American actress Marjorie King ("Marjorie" is equivalent to "Margarita" in Spanish). It was, at any rate, invented sometime around the 1950s.

Origin of the name aside, it's quite a good drink. Don't forget, of course, that strong spirits, lime, and sugar had been mixed for several decades previous to this, so the idea of mixing strong spirits and lime has, indeed, hung around for a while . . .

1 2/3 fl oz (50 ml) tequila
1 fl oz (30 ml) Cointreau
1 fl oz (30 ml) freshly-squeezed lime juice

Combine the ingredients in a shaker with ice; shake. Serve in a cocktail glass or "on the rocks." The salted rim is a must.

White Lady

It's difficult not to list this in the same breath as the margarita. The White Lady was invented by Harry Craddock and was part of *The Savoy Cocktail Book* (1930). A White Lady was also developed by Harry McElhone at Ciro's Club in 1919, but that one had Crème de Menthe in it, which was later exchanged for gin.

Harry McElhone was the same Harry who ran Harry's Bar in Paris, and was one of the biggest bartenders of his time and even something of a PR genius. One of his brilliant ideas was to market Harry's Bar in Parisian newspapers with a phonetic pronunciation of the street address, so that Americans would have an easier time reading it aloud. He also gave out luggage tacks to his guests, with "Return me to Harry's Bar, 5 Daunou" written on them, in case they happened to get too inebriated and required directions.

The White Lady is, in any case, an English invention, and it—like the margarita—falls into the category of strong (gin), sweet (Cointreau), and sour (lemon).

1 2/3 fl oz (50 ml) gin
1 fl oz (30 ml) Cointreau
1 fl oz (30 ml) freshly squeezed lemon juice

Combine the ingredients in a shaker with ice. Shake well. Serve in a cocktail glass with a sugared rim. You can garnish this with a maraschino cherry, if you like.

MARGARITA

Roy's Punch Out Toddy

Some of the really great classics come from the time back when man was still conquering land overseas with the help of wind and sail. Drinks like grog, the Gimlet, and the Pink Gin were all invented to keep tough, boorish men (I'm assuming that they were indeed men, by and large) from skimping on their vitamins while at sea.

This isn't the grog we're used to in Sweden—a liqueur and mixer, usually in the form of a carbonated drink. This is the rum-and-water variant that Vice Admiral Edward Vernon introduced to the English navy in August 21, 1740, and which became the standard a few years later. The foul-tasting water they had access to was simply diluted with rum to hide the unpleasant taste. Lemon, lime, and cinnamon were also used to make the water appetizing. Though at the time it was likely not yet known that lemon and lime helped fight scurvy, it was a fact that Vernon's men were healthier than other seamen. After a while, there was so much lime being consumed that the English seamen got the nickname "limeys." I personally don't have a favorite grog, but if you warm the water you get a toddy, and I do have a good version of that.

Roy Dymott was my grandfather's name, and he was in the English navy for the entirety of World War II. He was a professional boxer and swam like a blue whale. He was, and still is, my idol, and I'm proud to bear his name. This drink's based on his stories, and is a tribute to his time in the navy.

2 1/3 fl oz (70 ml) dark or gold rum
2 cinnamon sticks
1 pinch ginger
1 star anise
2/3 fl oz (20 ml) honey
1/2 lime, juice
3 1/3 fl oz (100 ml) water
nutmeg
(a pat of butter)

Combine everything but the nutmeg and rum in a saucepan; bring to a boil and then remove from the heat. Allow to sit and cool a few minutes. Pour the result into a mug (warmed first with a bit of boiling water), add the rum, and sprinkle a bit of nutmeg on top.

If you need to warm yourself up on a cold day, I recommend adding a good-sized pat of butter to the toddy. Let it melt and bind the mixture into a big, warm hug.

55

Gimlet

Another drink with ties to the English navy is the Gimlet. Some claim that the drink is named after the tool, which is a sort of awl. Others say that it was created by a medic in the navy by the name of Thomas D. Gimlette. In an attempt to get the seamen to drink more alcohol, as well as to make the required amount of anti-scurvy lime more palatable after a few weeks at sea, he mixed gin and lime. At that time, the limes were most commonly preserved in demerara rum, so it must have been quite the disorderly, messy mixture with a base of both gin and rum.

Several years later, in 1867, a man by the name of Lauchlan Rose found a way to preserve limes without alcohol, and in the same year, the Merchant Shipping Act introduced a mandatory lime ration for each and every sailor in the navy, to prevent scurvy. Rose's Lime, then, became more or less the standard for every sailor to drink.

*2 parts Plymouth Navy Strength Gin (or
    plain Plymouth Gin, for landlubbers)
1 part lime cordial (see page 12) or
    Rose's Lime*

Stir the gin and lime cordial in a mixing glass with ice. Serve in a cocktail glass.

Pink Gin

Angostura Bitters were developed by Dr. Johann Gottlieb Benjamin Siegert to help soldiers with their digestion; in 1830, he began delivering it to the English navy as well in order to combat sea sickness. Gin and bitters eventually became the standard for sailors.

2 1/3 fl oz (70 ml) Plymouth Navy Strength Gin or Plymouth Gin
7 splashes Angostura Bitters

Combine the ingredients in a mixing glass with ice; stir well. Serve in a cocktail glass and garnish with lemon peel.

Manhattan

The history of the Manhattan is a bit hazy. It came into being around 1860; one story is that it was created in New York's Manhattan Club, and another says it was made at a banquet held by Winston Churchill's mother. We do know that initially the proportions were inverted, i.e. two parts vermouth to one part rye whiskey. It was also in Jerry Thomas's *The Bar-Tender's Guide* from 1887.

Sweet? Dry? Or perhaps Perfect? This is another question you must ask yourself. A Sweet Manhattan is with sweet vermouth, a Dry is with dry vermouth, and a Perfect is with equal parts of both. This dry version was a Rat Pack favorite.

1 2/3 fl oz (50 ml) rye whiskey
2/3 fl oz (20 ml) vermouth
3 splashes Angostura Bitters

Combine the ingredients in a mixing glass with ice; stir. Serve in a martini glass.

I also made a variant that I called the Jerry Thomas Manhattan during my time at the Bakery; it's made as follows:

Jerry Thomas Manhattan

2 parts rye whiskey
1 part Carpano Classico
1/2 part Grand Marnier
3 splashes Orange Bitters
3 splashes Angostura Bitters
oil from 4 pieces of orange peel

Combine the ingredients in a mixing glass with ice; stir. Press the oil out of the four orange peels and onto the mixture; serve in a cold cocktail glass. Finish it off with one more small piece of orange peel and garnish with a maraschino cherry.

Hanky Panky

The first bar manager of The American Bar at the Savoy Hotel was a woman by the name of Ada Coleman, or "Coley", as she was known. She was at the helm during the introduction of cocktails to Europe, between 1903 and 1926. It's said that she really had quite the foul mouth, a real "broad."

She made this drink for a regular who wanted something with a bit of a special touch to it, and after a few days of experimenting, she arrived at this variant. When the regular tasted the drink, it's said that he burst out: "By Jove! This is the real hanky-panky!"

This drink has characteristics of both a Manhattan and a Negroni.

1 1/3 fl oz (40 ml) gin
2/3 fl oz (20 ml) sweet vermouth
1/3 fl oz (10 ml) Fernet Branca

Combine the ingredients in a mixing glass with ice. Stir well and serve in a cocktail glass. Top it off with a piece of orange peel.

Negroni

Greve Camillo Negroni invented this drink in Florence in 1919, when he ordered an Americano, but substituted the seltzer water for gin. There are endless ways to mix this one up. Try, for example, using bourbon instead of gin, and you've got yourself a Boulevardier—quite good!

3/4 fl oz (25 ml) gin
3/4 fl oz (25 ml) sweet vermouth
3/4 fl oz (25 ml) Campari

Combine the ingredients in a mixing glass with ice. Stir well and serve in a rocks glass with ice. Top it off with a piece of orange peel.

HANKY PANKY

LE VIEUX CARRÉ

Le Vieux Carré

"The old square" was the original name of the French Quarter, and it's also the name of this New Orleans classic. It was invented at the Hotel Monteleone by Victor Bergeron. The drink contains something from all the parts of the world that have come together in New Orleans: rye whiskey from America, brandy from Spain, Bénédictine from France, vermouth from Italy, and Angostura from the Caribbean.

2/3 fl oz (20 ml) rye whiskey
2/3 fl oz (20 ml) brandy
1/3 fl oz (10 ml) Bénédictine
    D.O.M.
2/3 fl oz (20 ml) sweet vermouth
3 splashes Peychaud's Bitters
3 splashes Angostura Bitters

Combnie the ingredients in a mixing glass with ice; stir. Serve in a whiskey glass with large ice cubes and garnish with a maraschino cherry.

Bijou Cocktail

The Bijou Cocktail was created by Harry Johnson, and can be found in his *Bartender's Manual* (1900). It's spicy, with a good kick, and really proves that Chartreuse is a liquor that works well in cocktails. Bijou means jewel, and if you mix this drink correctly, it gleams just like one.

3/4 fl oz (25 ml) gin
3/4 fl oz (25 ml) green
    Chartreuse
3/4 fl oz (25 ml) sweet
    vermouth
3 splashes Orange Bitters

Combine the ingredients in a mixing glass with ice. Stir well and serve in a cocktail glass with an ice cube. Top it off with a small piece of orange peel and a maraschino cherry.

Rock and Rye

For a long time, the Rock and Rye was recommended for all kinds of illnesses; there were even Rock and Rye tablets for children to combat coughs and colds. This was one of the first drinks we made at Little Quarter, and we've made many variants thereafter using flavored rock candy.

2 1/3 fl oz (70 ml) rye whiskey
1 fl oz (35 ml) rock candy syrup (see page 13)
3 pieces of orange peel
3 splashes Orange Bitters
3 splashes Angostura Bitters

Dissolve the rock candy syrup in the rye whiskey in a mixing glass. Press the oil out of two pieces of orange peel and into the mixture; add the bitters. Stir with ice. Serve in a rocks glass with ice, and a spoon on the side. Garnish with orange peel.

Blood and Sand

The Blood and Sand got its name from the film of the same name, which premiered in 1922, starring Rudolph Valentino and Rita Hayworth.

Normally, I'm a little allergic to Scotch whisky in cocktails, but this is one of maybe two or three that I really like. Substitute blood orange juice for regular orange juice when they're in season; it'll be a real treat.

1 1/3 fl oz (40 ml) Scotch single malt (a less smoky sort, like Ardbeg, for example)
2/3 fl oz (20 ml) red vermouth
1/2 fl oz (15 ml) Cheery Heering
1 2/3 fl oz (50 ml) freshly squeezed orange juice

Combine the ingredients in a shaker with ice; shake. Serve in a cocktail glass and garnish with a piece of orange peel.

Tequila Sunrise (Bloody)

While I'm at it, there is one thing I must say: if you want to make another real classic but want to give it a little twist, there are few things that beat a Tequila Sunrise with freshly squeezed blood oranges.

2 1/3 fl oz (70 ml) 100% Agave Tequila
2 1/3 fl oz (70 ml) freshly-squeezed blood orange juice
1 fl oz (30 ml) Grenadine

Combine the tequila and juice in a shaker with ice; shake. Pour into a tall glass with ice and top with Grenadine to make the "sun rise." Garnish with a maraschino cherry and a piece of orange peel.

BLOOD AND SAND

I LIKE TO SHAKE MY JUICE DRINKS—THAT IS, I EVEN SHAKE SCREWDRIVERS WHEN I THINK THE RESULT WILL BE NOTICEABLY BETTER. YOU GET A SMOOTH, EVEN CHILL THROUGHOUT THE WHOLE DRINK.

Moscow Mule

The story of how the Moscow Mule came to be sounds like a classic joke. Three guys are sitting in a bar, the year is 1941, and the bar's called the Cock 'n' Bull Tavern on Sunset Strip in Los Angeles. It was Jack Morgan, the owner of the Cock 'n' Bull Tavern and the producer of ginger beer; John G. Martin, owner of Heublein Brothers, Inc. and importer of Smirnoff; and finally Rudolph Kunnet, manager for Pierre Smirnoff, Heublein's vodka division. One murky evening, the not-so-advanced mixture was created and dubbed the Moscow Mule—Moscow, since vodka is seen as a Russian product, and Mule being a name for a category of drinks with citrus and ginger beer. Try it first without bitters, and then with, if you want a good example of just what they can do for a drink.

Copper mugs were a sales gimmick, and the drink was used to promote Smirnoff in bars. It's said to have contributed to the Yanks' switching from gin to vodka as their "white spirit of choice."

2 1/3 fl oz (70 ml) Smirnoff
1/2 lime, juice
3 splashes Angostura Bitters
2 1/3-2 3/4 fl oz (70-80 ml) ginger beer

Build the drink on ice in a copper mug. If you don't have a copper mug, an Old Fashioned glass also works nicely.

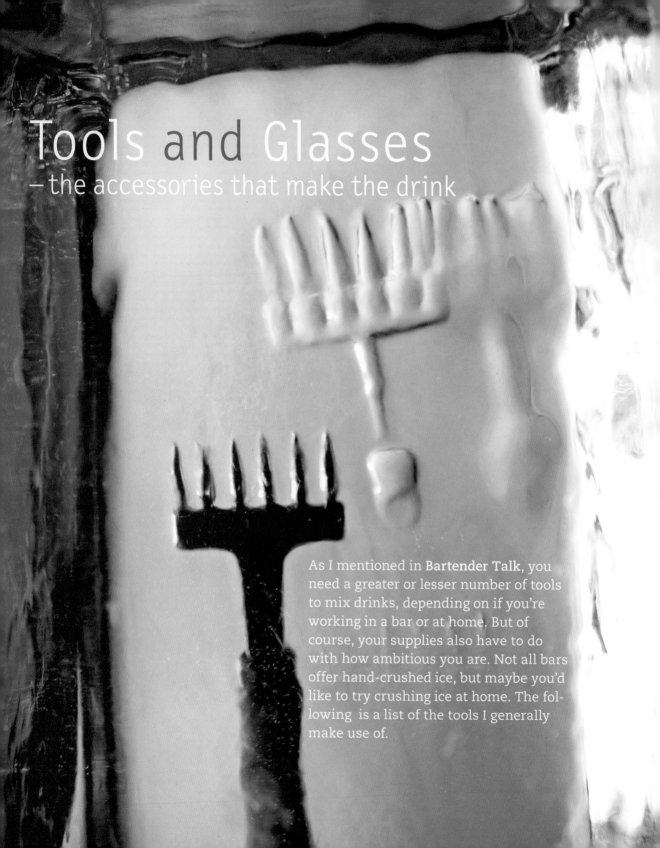

Tools and Glasses
– the accessories that make the drink

As I mentioned in **Bartender Talk**, you need a greater or lesser number of tools to mix drinks, depending on if you're working in a bar or at home. But of course, your supplies also have to do with how ambitious you are. Not all bars offer hand-crushed ice, but maybe you'd like to try crushing ice at home. The following is a list of the tools I generally make use of.

ICE PICK

PEELER

BAR SPOONS

JULEP STRAINER

FINE SIEVE

JUICER

STRAINER

JIGGER

71

JIGGER or **MEASURING GLASS** The measurements on them don't make much of a difference; the important part is getting the proportions right.

BAR SPOON A spoon with a long handle for stirring ingredients in a mixing glass or shaker.

MIXING GLASS A thicker sort of glass with a pouring spout, for chilling drinks that are stirred rather than shaken. As a general rule, you could say that you stir ingredients that mix easily with each other, and which, as a rule, result in clear drinks.

SHAKER I use a two-piece Boston Shaker with both pieces made of tin, partially because it chills the drink well, but also because there's a high risk of the glass shattering from the ice we're shaking. A shaker is used to blend ingredients that don't mix so easily naturally, without using a bit more force to "bond" them together. As a rule, these are mostly "cloudy cocktails," turbid drinks with, for example, fruit or eggs.

FRUIT KNIFE or **TOMATO KNIFE** A small, serrated knife is the easiest thing to use for cutting fruits and peels.

STRAINER (COCKTAIL SIEVE) Used to separate ice and liquid. Sometimes, you'll also want to use a fine sieve to separate smaller things that shouldn't end up in the glass, such as the mint in a Southside (see page 100).

ICE TONGS

ICE KNIFE A cheap, coarsely-serrated bread knife is perfect for cutting ice into smaller pieces, and also gives a nice finish to the ice pieces in the glass.

ICE PICK, CHISEL, MALLET Used to cut a large block of ice into smaller pieces that are easy to work with.

CHAIN SAW If you're like me and you work with 275-pound blocks of ice, a chain saw helps quite a bit. This should never be oiled, and should always be stored with the blade facing downward, so the water from the ice doesn't seep into the motor and cause it to rust.

LEWIS BAG A canvas bag used for crushing ice. At home, you can just as easily wrap the ice in a dish towel and then either crush the ice with a mallet or hit it against a hard floor (real parquet!).

JUICER Manual or mechanical; whatever works best for you. At Little Quarter, we do things by hand.

BITTERS BOTTLES When I work with bitters, we store them in bitters bottles, but all bitters come in bottles that dispense drops in one way or another.

SUGAR

, LJ, EGG WHITE

, GRENADINE (PB) (AB)

MON, SUGAR, SODA

45

Little Quarter

There's a jungle of glasses out there, and few things are as cool as using all sorts of vintage glasses. When I owned f/l Cocktail Bar, a little members-only bar that fit only 40 people at a time, I'd spend some time every Monday going around and searching second-hand stores for glasses. If you're making yourself a bar at home, I think this is really the way to go. If you're running a larger bar, it's not particularly realistic or economical to think that you'll be able to handle everything with vintage glasses, so I've picked out a few basic ones that I think do the job.

WINE GLASS Used for cobblers, like a Sherry Cobbler, and, of course, wine.

OLD FASHIONED GLASS or **LARGE ROCKS GLASS** Used for cocktails that contain ice, and carbonated, iced drinks, such as an Old Fashioned or a Gin & Tonic.

WHISKEY GLASS or **SMALL ROCKS GLASS** Used for cocktails without ice but that still need to be served in a more solid, steady glass, like a Sazerac, or whiskey served "neat."

COUPETTE or **COCKTAIL GLASS** Used for "cloudy cocktails," i.e. cocktails with fruit, like a Mardi Gras, champagne-based cocktails, and champagne.

HIGHBALL GLASS Used for fizzes like a Morning Glory Fizz or Collins, and drinks with juice on ice, such as a Screwdriver.

MARTINI GLASS or **V-SHAPED GLASS** Used for "clear cocktails," clear drinks without fruit, like The Hearst.

Besides the glasses in the picture, you'll also want a mug with a handle for serving warm drinks. Another glass that's really useful to have is a smaller wine glass or wine-tasting glass—I use these for flips and a few other drinks, such as the Brandy Crusta.

Champagne—
cocktails
and cobblers

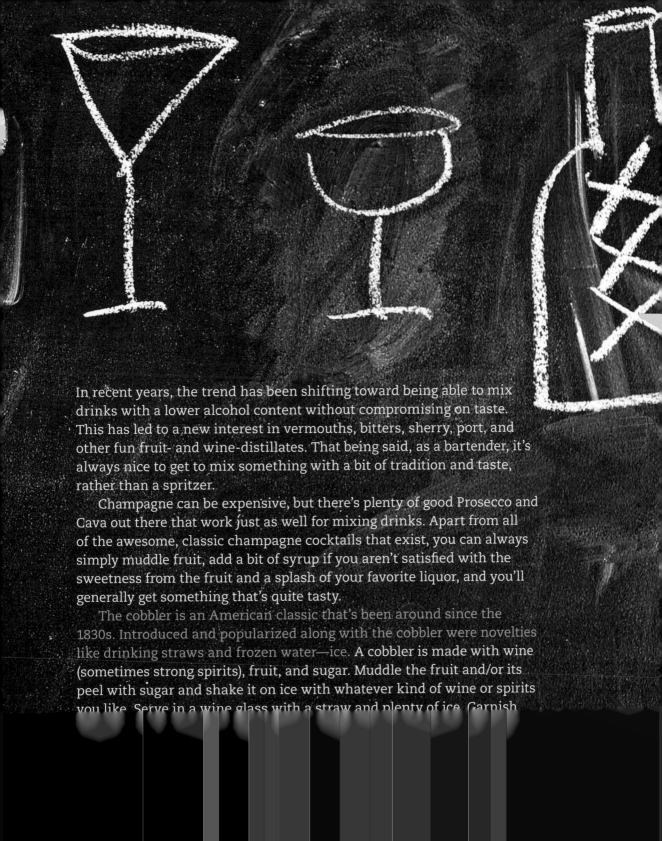

In recent years, the trend has been shifting toward being able to mix drinks with a lower alcohol content without compromising on taste. This has led to a new interest in vermouths, bitters, sherry, port, and other fun fruit- and wine-distillates. That being said, as a bartender, it's always nice to get to mix something with a bit of tradition and taste, rather than a spritzer.

Champagne can be expensive, but there's plenty of good Prosecco and Cava out there that work just as well for mixing drinks. Apart from all of the awesome, classic champagne cocktails that exist, you can always simply muddle fruit, add a bit of syrup if you aren't satisfied with the sweetness from the fruit and a splash of your favorite liquor, and you'll generally get something that's quite tasty.

The cobbler is an American classic that's been around since the 1830s. Introduced and popularized along with the cobbler were novelties like drinking straws and frozen water—ice. A cobbler is made with wine (sometimes strong spirits), fruit, and sugar. Muddle the fruit and/or its peel with sugar and shake it on ice with whatever kind of wine or spirits you like. Serve in a wine glass with a straw and plenty of ice. Garnish

A real brunch classic that's saved many a Sunday. It's called a Mimosa in the United States and Buck's Fizz in England. Regardless of which name you prefer, orange juice and champagne are very good friends.

1 part freshly-squeezed orange juice
1 part champagne

Mix and serve in a champagne glass. Or, if you're like me and thirsty, in a wine glass with ice.

80 mimosa

Breck and Brace

This drink comes from William Boothby's *The World's Drinks and How To Mix Them* (1908). Buck and Breck is another variant attributed to Jerry Thomas, but he used a splash of absinthe and two splashes of Angostura Bitters in his.

Breck and Brace travels up and down the list at Little Quarter—it's a flavorful and simple party drink that always gets things going.

1 part champagne
1 part cognac
1 small handful of
   sugar

Moisten the inside of a coupette—the champagne glass of the 1920s—with a splash of champagne, and sprinkle it with sugar. Stir the cognac in a mixing glass with ice; pour into the coupette. Top off with ice-cold champagne. Knock it back!

Champagne Cocktail

Mixing strong spirits with champagne is one of the best combinations, and such drinks have been around for quite some time. Mark Twain mentions the Champagne Cocktail in his first book *The Innocents Abroad* from 1869.

I can only agree with Churchill when he said that champagne ought to be cold, dry, and free! The original from Jerry Thomas's *The Bar-Tender's Guide* (1887) didn't contain brandy.

1 fl oz (35 ml) brandy
1 cube of raw sugar
4 splashes Angostura Bitters
champagne

VARIANT

Another way to mix this drink is to build it directly on ice in a wine glass, with simple syrup instead of the sugar cube. But then it must be drunk quickly, or the ice will water it down.

Soak the sugar cube with Angostura Bitters. Set it in the glass and pour in the brandy. Fill the glass with champagne and garnish with lemon peel.

Champagne Cobbler

4 fl oz (120 ml) champagne
3 pieces of orange peel
2 pieces of lemon peel
3 pieces of grapefruit peel
1 fl oz (30 ml) simple syrup

Vigorously shake the fruit peels and syrup in a shaker. Pour in a third of the champagne and shake with ice; be careful with the fizz. Pour into a wine glass filled with ice and top off with the rest of the champagne. Decorate with fruit.

CHAMPAGNE COBBLER

Sherry Cobbler

The cobbler was apparently so popular at one point that Jerry Thomas included seven variants of it in his book from 1887. These were the Sherry Cobbler, Champagne Cobbler, Catawba Cobbler (an American grape; rosé wine works as an alternative), Hock Cobbler (Hock is a collective term for German white wines from the Rhine area, and perhaps derogative), Claret Cobbler (once again lumping together Bordeaux wines), Sauterne Cobbler, and Whiskey Cobbler. The greatest of them all was the Sherry Cobbler.

4 fl oz (120 ml) dry sherry
3 pieces of orange peel
2 pieces of lemon peel
3 pieces of grapefruit peel
1 fl oz (30 ml) simple syrup

Vigorously shake the fruit peels and syrup in a shaker. Pour in the sherry and shake with ice. Pour into a wine glass filled with ice; decorate with fruit. Don't forget a straw!

Bourbon Cobbler

This is a cobbler with an extra bit of kick; otherwise, the cobbler is perfect for hot summer evenings when you're thirsty and want lots to drink without needing to be sent home at midnight. If you're very thirsty, I'd recommend choosing a variant without strong spirits.

1 2/3 fl oz (50 ml) bourbon
2/3 fl oz (20 ml) Maraschino liquor
3 pieces of orange peel
2 pieces of lemon peel
3 pieces of grapefruit peel
1/2 fl oz (15 ml) simple syrup

Thoroughly shake the fruit peels and syrup in a shaker. Pour in bourbon and Maraschino liquor; shake with ice. Serve in a wine glass with ice and decorate with fruit.

85

SHERRY COBBLER

Ice
– the best and neatest way to chill a drink

Ice at the bar is a given, and getting to enjoy an ice-cold cocktail feels like it's a basic human right, but that hasn't always been the case. Everything started with two well-to-do brothers from the Tudor line in Boston, who were having a picnic while enjoying such luxuries as cold drinks and ice cream. They jokingly began discussing the idea of trying to deliver ice to people on a large scale. This discussion must have ignited a spark in one of the brothers, Frederic Tudor, because thirty years later he was delivering 180 tons of ice halfway around the globe, and adopted the nickname "Ice King."

When nobody in Boston was willing to support the brothers' harebrained scheme to deliver ice to warmer climes, Frederic Tudor and his brother William got together some funds and bought a ship, and in 1806, a boat full of ice finally left New England for the Caribbean. They made it there with the entire cargo, though nobody seemed interested in buying what the "Yanks" had to offer, and after this bad start (and that's putting it nicely), William decided to leave. Frederic, on the other hand, was confident that if he could just get people to taste a nice, cold drink, they wouldn't be able to live without one.

Said and done, Frederic persevered, and around 1810, people finally began to take an interest in his business venture. Unfortunately, a trade embargo, war, and a series of personal tragedies all hit at the same time, which ended up bankrupting the Tudor family. Frederic found himself in trouble with the law on numerous occasions, and was forced to lie low to avoid the debt collectors. But with a strong belief that started to look more and more like an obsession, he continued to travel the country, convincing bartenders to offer cold drinks at the same price as the not-so-cold ones and see what the customers preferred, while also training chefs and restaurateurs in the production of ice cream and other frozen delicacies. It's said that people didn't even know they needed cold drinks, or ice itself, for that matter, but when Tudor got them to try it, there were few who could manage without it.

Between 1821 and 1833, Tudor expanded his business as the demand continued to grow. With the help of new techniques and a few new associates who developed the method of "harvesting" the ice, so to speak (a difficult job that resulted in a number of deaths and crushing injuries), he got his name of the "Ice King" when he, in 1833, delivered 180 tons of ice from New Hampshire to the English colonists in Calcutta.

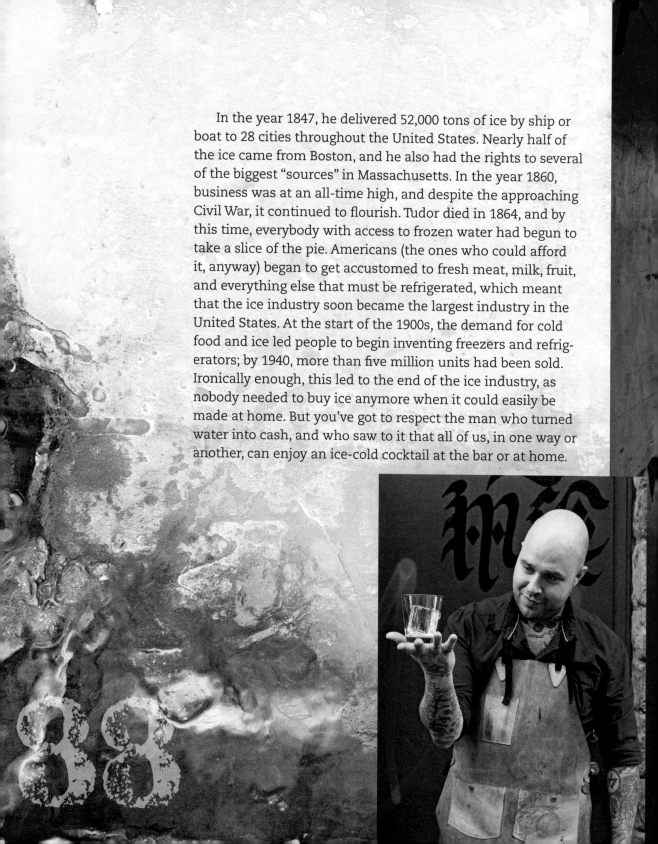

In the year 1847, he delivered 52,000 tons of ice by ship or boat to 28 cities throughout the United States. Nearly half of the ice came from Boston, and he also had the rights to several of the biggest "sources" in Massachusetts. In the year 1860, business was at an all-time high, and despite the approaching Civil War, it continued to flourish. Tudor died in 1864, and by this time, everybody with access to frozen water had begun to take a slice of the pie. Americans (the ones who could afford it, anyway) began to get accustomed to fresh meat, milk, fruit, and everything else that must be refrigerated, which meant that the ice industry soon became the largest industry in the United States. At the start of the 1900s, the demand for cold food and ice led people to begin inventing freezers and refrigerators; by 1940, more than five million units had been sold. Ironically enough, this led to the end of the ice industry, as nobody needed to buy ice anymore when it could easily be made at home. But you've got to respect the man who turned water into cash, and who saw to it that all of us, in one way or another, can enjoy an ice-cold cocktail at the bar or at home.

Ice Philosophy

When it comes to ice, and what type of ice you should use, there are a great many opinions as to what makes the best cocktail. I use ice that is completely clear and mechanically produced in a machine called a Clinebell. It takes three days to produce a block; and in Sweden we use plain tap water to make the ice, since our water is nice and clean to begin with. In order to make the ice completely clear, the Clinebell machine has small fans that pump the water around in the tank while it is slowly frozen from underneath. Because air is lighter than water, the air bubbles are pushed up as the ice freezes, making an ice block without any air in it, or so-called mechanically clear ice.

When an ice block arrives at the bar, it weighs 275 pounds and measures 3 x 1 x 1.5 feet. In order to be able to work with the block without it cracking, it gets packed up and is allowed to thaw for roughly two hours. When the ice has thawed and has become completely clear, it gets cut into smaller pieces that are easier to work with. From here, there are various ways to proceed, depending on what sort of glasses you're using and what kind of drink-mixing philosophy you adhere to. Some people like to make cubes, diamonds, and other crazy creations. I use a more traditional method, restraining myself to one larger piece of ice for the short glasses I like to serve drinks in, two smaller ones for the tall glasses, and one large one for shaking. I usually use a piece of ice that's exactly large enough to fit in the shaker.

At Little Quarter, we use deoxygenated ice, as we think that it cools the drink better without watering it down as much as a plain ice cube, but also because it fits in with our bar's concept. We're a "no shortcut bar" where it's all about producing and managing as much as possible in-house. Here, we press and flavor everything we can right in the bar, and preferably no sooner than when it's ordered. Ice, too, has its natural place in this system.

There's one other reason too, and that's the fact that there is nothing more beautiful than a hand-cut piece of ice in a glass of bourbon. To a bartender (or at least for me and my colleagues), the sound of the hard ice against the side of the glass is like hearing the ice cream truck on a summer day back when you were eight years old. We love working with this ice, and we're proud of the effort we put into its preparation, as well as of the perfect piece of ice melting slowly in the customer's glass.

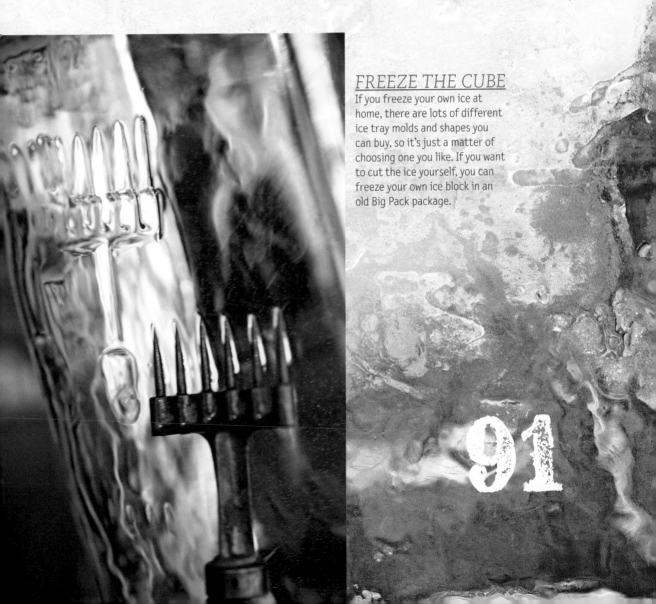

FREEZE THE CUBE

If you freeze your own ice at home, there are lots of different ice tray molds and shapes you can buy, so it's just a matter of choosing one you like. If you want to cut the ice yourself, you can freeze your own ice block in an old Big Pack package.

91

Sours

PEGU CLUB, P. 107

A sour is a drink with strong spirits, lemon, sugar, and water (ice), and is perhaps the most popular type of drink. There are endless variations, including using lime instead of lemon, all the different kinds of sweet and spiced liquors there are, bitters, flavored syrups, eggs, milk, cream, spices, and fruits. Everything works with a sour base, as long as you experiment a bit to find a balance (everyone who has tasted a perfectly balanced sour knows what I'm talking about). You can guarantee that anybody who has tasted a poorly balanced sour also knows how important this balance and feeling are when mixing such a thirst-quencher.

Of course, a sour should be made with fresh lemon or lime juice.

Whiskey Sour

This is the most popular sour. I use egg whites in my sour, which is a bit more European. I enjoy the silky-smooth feeling the egg white provides.

2 1/3 fl oz (70 ml) bourbon
1 1/3 fl oz (40 ml) freshly squeezed
*   lemon juice*
1 fl oz (30 ml) simple syrup
3/4 fl oz (25 ml) egg whites
4 splashes Angostura Bitters

Combine the ingredients in a shaker in the same order as above. Dry-shake, and then shake with ice. Serve in a rocks glass with ice, and garnish with a lemon peel and a maraschino cherry.

New York Sour

A good variant of the Whiskey Sour is the New York Sour, where the bourbon is replaced with rye whiskey, and the drink's topped off with a dash of red wine. Pour the wine over the back of a bar spoon so the wine will layer on top like a little roof for the drink. "It gives the drink a hell of a 'snap,'" as a Chicago bartender said back in 1880. I don't know why the drink ended up being called a New York Sour, but it's certainly tasty.

WHISKEY SOUR

95

Pisco Sour

Pisco is the national drink of Peru and Chile, and is a grape distillate. There's considerable debate about which country is pisco's home-land, and where the best pisco is made—Peru or Chile. In any case, I have a few associates at work who bring pisco back from Peru when they visit family there, and I can say that the pisco they bring back kicks the ass of anything I've ever tried here at home. Though, better and better products are coming to Sweden, so we can either wait and see what happens, or take a trip to Chile and Peru and do a taste test ourselves. As I'm writing this, I realizing that I'm going to take some shit from my Chilean friends, so I'll simply say that it's a dead heat for me.

A Pisco Sour with Amargo's Peruvian Bitters is hard to beat on a hot summer day. Amargo Bitters are quite difficult to get a hold of, but I think this drink works quite well without the bitters, too.

2 1/3 fl oz (70 ml) pisco
1 1/3 fl oz (40 ml) freshly squeezed
    lemon juice
3/4 fl oz (25 ml) simple syrup
3/4 fl oz (25 ml) egg whites
(optionally, a few splashes of Amargo
    Bitters)

Combine the ingredients in a shaker, in the same order as above. Dry-shake, and then shake with ice. Serve in a smaller rocks glass or a sour glass.

I USUALLY PRESS THE OIL OUT OF A LEMON PEEL AND ONTO THE DRINK TO GIVE IT A BIT MORE "NOSE."

97

Aviation

At one time, it felt like all we ever made at f/l Cocktail Bar (the Bakery) was the Aviation. I had managed to track down violet liqueur, which had become quite difficult to find, and people went crazy over the old-yet-new taste. The drink was in Hugo Ensslin's *Recipes for Mixed Drinks* (1916). It was also to be found in Harry Craddock's *The Savoy Cocktail Book* (1930), but by that time, the violet had fallen away, and the drink was a much sharper creature. I prefer it with Crème de Violette, which rounds it off and makes the flavor very interesting.

1 2/3 fl oz (50 ml) Miller's Gin
1/2 fl oz (15 ml) Maraschino liqueur
1/3 fl oz (10 ml) Crème de Violette
1 fl oz (35 ml) freshly squeezed lemon juice

Combine the ingredients in a shaker, in the same order as above. Shake on ice and serve in a cocktail glass. Garnish with a maraschino cherry.

FONDÉE EN 1836

...queur de

Violette

...ND BRIOTTET

...FRANCE

..., ALCOOL, AROME VIOLETTE,

...L11135

18% vol

Southside

There are three different stories tied to this drink, which I've attempted to summarize here:

The first, which seems the most credible, is that the drink was created at the Southside Sportsmen's Club in Long Island. It's said to have been developed from the Mint Julep, which people practically drank buckets of, and when people got tired of it, bartenders came up with new variants. That particular variant, however, was a Collins variant with seltzer water, which also works well.

Another story is that it was created at a speakeasy by the name of Jack and Charlie's during Prohibition in New York. Jack and Charlie's moved around quite a bit, finally ending up on 21 West and 52nd Street, where it changed its name to the 21 Club.

The last story is that it comes from Chicago and the period when gangsters fought for control of the alcohol trade during Prohibition. The Southside Gang was led by Frankie McErlane, who was the first to use a Tommy gun during an argument. The liquor they sold was said to have tasted so bad that bartenders had to add sugar, lemon, and sometimes also mint in order to hide the unpleasant flavor—and Simsalabim, there's our Southside. The story sounds a bit ridiculous, but it's kind of fun to imagine McErlane and Capone struggling for supremacy while sipping Southsides.

MINT

Try to buy fresh mint in bunches from your grocer. You'll get much more out of fresh mint than the jars you can find in supermarkets. At my bar, we use spearmint.

2 1/3 fl oz (70 ml) gin
a small handful of mint
1 fl oz (30 ml) simple syrup
1 1/3 fl oz (40 ml) freshly squeezed lemon
    juice

Vigorously shake the mint with the syrup in a shaker. Add the gin and lemon; shake with ice. Next, double-strain the drink—that is, use a fine sieve in addition to your usual strainer to remove any extra mint when pouring the drink into the glass. Serve in a cocktail glass and garnish with a sprig of mint.

100

Honeysuckle

This drink is from David Embury's *The Fine Art of Mixing Drinks* (1948). Honey is excellent to use instead of sugar for sweetening drinks, and works really well with most kinds of spirits. Try mixing a bit of water with honey and whatever liquor you like, and then add a touch of your favorite bitters for a truly delicious cocktail.

2 1/3 fl oz (70 ml) light rum
1 fl oz (30 ml) honey water (see page 13)
1 1/3 fl oz (40 ml) freshly squeezed lime juice

Combine the ingredients in a shaker in the same order as above. Shake with ice and serve in a cocktail glass.

Clover Club

The Clover Club was a gentlemen's club at the Bellevue-Stratford Hotel in Philadelphia. This is a drink I usually make for people who tell me they don't like gin. When you work at a bar that presses its own juices, you rarely have cranberry juice, since cranberries are expensive to juice and are somewhat difficult to obtain year-round, which means you can't always mix a Cosmopolitan. In such a case, the Clover Club is the perfect drink to recommend instead.

1 2/3 fl oz (50 ml) gin
2/3 fl oz (20 ml) dry vermouth
2/3 fl oz (20 ml) raspberry syrup (see page 13)
1 1/3 fl oz (40 ml) freshly squeezed lemon juice
2/3 fl oz (20 ml) egg whites

Combine the ingredients in a shaker in the same order as above. Dry-shake and then shake on ice. Serve in a cocktail glass and press the oil from a piece of lemon peel on top.

Pendennis Cocktail

The Pendennis Club is a gentlemen's club in Louisville, Kentucky, which is perhaps best known for being the place where the Old Fashioned was supposedly invented. But they can also boast of this little concoction, which is a real "crowd-pleaser." There's something special about apricot in drinks.

1 ½ fl oz (45 ml) gin
2/3 fl oz (20 ml) apricot brandy
3/4 fl oz (25 ml) freshly squeezed lime juice
2 splashes Peychaud's Bitters

Combine the ingredients in a shaker and shake with ice. Serve in a cocktail glass.

CLOVER CLUB

100

PEGU CLUB

Pegu Club

Yet another cocktail named after a gentlemen's club—this time a British one from the 1920s and colonial Burma. The drink came from there and made its way into Harry McElhone's *Barflies and Cocktails* (1927). Note that there's very little lime juice in this one; it's a spicy, quick drink that's unbelievably cool and refreshing on hot days.

1 1/2 fl oz (45 ml) gin
3/4 (25 ml) Cointreau
2/3 fl oz (20 ml) freshly squeezed lime juice
3 splashes Angostura Bitters
(optionally, Orange Bitters)

Combine the ingredients in a shaker; shake with ice. Serve in a cocktail glass.

The Last Word

A drink that originated during Prohibition at a Detroit gentlemen's club known as the Detroit Athletic Club. This drink had largely been forgotten, but was revived when a bartender by the name of Murray Stenson dusted it off for the opening of the Zig Zag Café in Seattle, in 2004, and has been a bartender favorite ever since.

3/4 fl oz (25 ml) gin
3/4 fl oz (25 ml) green Chartreuse
3/4 fl oz (25 ml) Maraschino liquor
3/4 fl oz (25 ml) freshly
*   squeezed lime juice*

Combine the ingredients in a shaker; shake with ice. Serve in a cocktail glass.

Corpse Reviver no. 2

The Corpse Reviver is actually a drink category in and of itself, made up of drinks that were designed to cure hangovers and were supposed to be consumed in the morning. Harry Craddock, the legendary Savoy bartender who invented this variant, recommended knocking back four of these in quick succession as a hangover cure—ah, if only we could have joined him back then!

Corpse Reviver no. 1 is a variant with equal parts brandy, calvados, and sweet vermouth, and Corpse Reviver no. 3 is a variant with Swedish punch instead of Cointreau.

Personally, I like the second variant best, and it's the one people request the most. The others are a bit more "premium," but can be fun to know.

3/4 fl oz (25 ml) gin
3/4 fl oz (25 ml) Lillet
3/4 fl oz (25 ml) Cointreau
3/4 fl oz (25 ml) freshly squeezed lemon juice
a small bar spoon of absinthe

Combine the ingredients in a shaker; shake with ice. Pour into a cocktail glass and press the oil from a piece of orange peel on top.

Corpse reviver

109

The Millionaire Cocktail

The Millionaire Cocktail exists as several variants; this one comes from *The Savoy Cocktail Book* (1930) and is the one I like the most. Harry Craddock, who wrote the book, simplified many recipes because of the difficulty in acquiring some kinds of spirits in Europe, though I really do like his simplified cocktails, and for me, Savoy is a real bible.

1 1/3 fl oz (40 ml) rum
2/3 fl oz (20 ml) Sloe Gin
1/2 fl oz (15 ml) apricot brandy
1 fl oz (35 ml) freshly squeezed lime juice
1/2 fl oz (15 ml) Grenadine

Combine the ingredients in a shaker; shake with ice. Pour into a cocktail glass and garnish with a maraschino cherry.

ONAIRE COCKTAIL

~~~~~~~~~~~

SLOE GIN,

RANDY, LIME,

INE

Spirits
—the foundation of a perfect cocktai

When you mix drinks, you've obviously got to have access to a wide range of spirits, but that range isn't necessarily as wide you might think. It's not always easy to know what you should choose, so I thought I'd talk a little about the most important kinds of spirits, and what makes them special.

BOURBON

For it to be called bourbon, the whiskey must be produced in the United States. It must be made from at least 51% corn, and be aged in new barrels of charred American oak. Bourbon gets its flavor and color from being stored in such barrels. The taste is generally a little sweet, with notes of vanilla, caramel, and oak. It can be perceived as a bit spicy, and good bourbon always has a nice kick to it and warms your throat.

RYE WHISKEY

The only interesting rye whiskey is the rye whiskey that comes from the United States. American rye whiskey must contain 51% rye, and be aged in new barrels of charred American oak. It's usually described as being fruitier and spicier than bourbon.

I find that a drink can be perceived as more dry when using rye whiskey, while bourbon gives it a sweeter taste. The Old Fashioned and Manhattan were originally made with rye whiskey.

SCOTCH WHISKY

There aren't that many good Scotch cocktails in my opinion, but for those who would like to delve deeper into the subject, there have been thousands of books written about Scotch. What I can tell you is this: when you want to mix Scotch cocktails, use a classic Highland single malt that's not too smoky. This is because blended Scotch wasn't around until much later, and most drinks that came around since Prohibition were mixed with a single malt.

spirits

GIN

Gin is a distilled spirit flavored primarily with juniper and coriander; that being said, every brand has its own variations with, for example, citrus, cinnamon, bergamot, almond, bitter almond, iris root, angelica root, etc. The list goes on and new variants are constantly showing up. There are a few different versions of gin:

LONDON DRY GIN is the most common variant, with a dry taste and a clear, distinct note of juniper. It's called "dry" to distinguish it from Old Tom Gin, which is sweet.

PLYMOUTH GIN is a milder sort of London Dry that can seem a bit sweeter.

GENEVER This is the original from the Netherlands that was copied by the English. It's spiced with, among other things, juniper or juniper oil, coriander, and angelica root, and has an oily taste from being aged in spruce barrels.

OLD TOM GIN is a sugar-sweetened variant that was used extensively in the United States before Prohibition, and is often found in original recipes for a number of classic cocktails.

GOLDEN GIN is aged in oak barrels to give it a golden color.

RUM

Rum is a distilled spirit produced with molasses from cane sugar or fermented sugarcane juice. There is an abundance of rum variants, but if we're talking about mixing drinks, there are really only three interesting ones, and these are light, gold, and aged rum, to simplify things considerably.

I'm a sucker for Havana and gladly stick to their products when mixing cocktails. Añejo Blanco and the three-year-old variant are unbeatable in cocktails, and if you're after a darker, smoother variant, their Reserve is fierce. Sometimes, it just doesn't need to be any more difficult than that.

BRANDY/COGNAC

Grape distillate produced in the proper region of France, i.e. Cognac, can be called just that; otherwise, it's called brandy. The wine is fermented and aged in oak barrels, where it acquires notes of vanilla, caramel, and oak itself, among other things.

Brandy is produced from distilled wine.

Pisco is also a grape distillate, produced primarily in Peru and Chile.

TEQUILA/MEZCAL

Tequila is produced from agave tequilana, and in order to be called tequila, it must meet certain criteria that are set by the Consejo Regulador del Tequila. Put simply, it must come from certain regions and be produced from tequila agave. It must be produced in the state of Jalisco or certain parts of the states of Tamaulipas, Guanajuato, Michoacan, and Nayarit.

Mezcal is a collective name for spirits produced from other species of the agave family, and isn't quite as strictly regulated—more rock 'n' roll, so to speak.

There are two variants of tequila. Tequila that is not 100% agave is simply called tequila or mixto, and must contain at least 51% tequila agave. Then we have Tequila 100% Agave, whose name says it all. You can guess which kind you should use if you have a choice . . .

For drink mixing, I stick to either a Blanco (non-aged) or a Reposado (aged in oak barrels for two months to a year). If you'd like to learn more about tequila, I suggest dropping by Little Quarter and asking for my associate, Björn Kjellberg, who is northern Europe's savviest tequila maestro, and a fierce bartender.

Flips and Egg Nog drinks

Egg drinks are a category all their own, and there exist both warm and cool variants. During the early 1800s, they were consumed daily in the United States as well as in Europe. At the time of their invention, they were among the most luxurious things you could drink, as they included both eggs and the expensive nutmeg for spice.

In recent years, the flip has been revived and is increasingly in demand. The flip is served cold, and when properly made, it's incredibly smooth and tastes like the most delicious cake batter. At the beginning, and here we're talking about the 1600s, a flip was a mixture of beer, rum, and sugar that was heated with a red-hot iron, which caused the mixture to bubble ("flip"), hence the name. Over time, the beer disappeared, more sugar was added, and eggs somehow made their way into the picture. I've never found a proper explanation for the eggs, but that's how it is. The warm variants have always been natural choices to serve around Christmas and New Year's.

Coffee Cocktail

A classic recipe from Jerry Thomas's *The Bar-Tender's Guide* from 1887. Jerry didn't use any bitters in his version, but I usually add in a few splashes of Angostura Bitters, since I feel that it gives the drink a bit more "body."

1 fl oz (35 ml) Ruby Port
1 fl oz (35 ml) brandy
1 egg
3/4 fl oz (25 ml) simple syrup
(optionally, Angostura Bitters)
nutmeg

Combine the ingredients in a shaker; shake with ice. Serve in a small wine glass without ice and sprinkle a bit of nutmeg on top.

smooth as silk and absolutely wonderful

118

New York Flip

My favorite flip—perhaps the only one I really like, come to think of it. Initially, the difference between a flip and an eggnog was that the eggnog contained cream or milk; since then, this distinction has disappeared, and many bartenders add cream to their flips to make them creamier.

I like my flips without cream.

1 1/3 fl oz (40 ml) bourbon
1 fl oz (30 ml) Ruby Port
1 egg
3/4 fl oz (25 ml) simple syrup
nutmeg

Combine the ingredients in a shaker; shake with ice. Serve in a small wine glass without ice. Sprinkle nutmeg on top.

Egg Nog

The drink that says "Merry Christmas!" can be served warm or cold.
I prefer it strong and warm, with lots of nutmeg. You can play around
a bit with the spirits in this drink. Experiment, for example, by trying
tequila instead of rum or cognac.

> 1 2/3 fl oz (50 ml) cognac
> 2/3 fl oz (20 ml) dark rum
> 1 fl oz (30 ml) simple syrup
> 1 egg
> 1 2/3 fl oz (50 ml) milk
> nutmeg

THE COLD VARIANT:
Mix the ingredients in a shaker; shake with ice. Pour into a
wine glass with crushed ice and sprinkle nutmeg on top.

THE WARM VARIANT:
Combine the spirits, syrup, and egg in a shaker; dry-shake
without ice. Pour the mixture into a cup that's been warmed
with hot water; fill with warm milk. Sprinkle nutmeg on top.

Tom and Jerry

After referencing Jerry Thomas as much as I have, it's difficult for me not to mention this drink. The Tom and Jerry is occasionally called the Jerry Thomas, and was one of the drinks he was most known for throughout his lifetime, despite not actually inventing it. What he did do was popularize the drink, and sometimes that's enough to "claim" something. Jerry Thomas became widely known during his lifetime for his wisdom and technique behind the bar counter and as a showman of rank. He also wrote one of the very first cocktail manuals for other bartenders, *How to Mix Drinks*, which was published in 1862.

The idea is to mix a large batch and serve it over the course of the evening. Here is a recipe I made use of during a Christmas party, and is enough for five to eight people, depending on the size of the mugs.

FOR THE BATTER:
4 eggs
2 3/4 fl oz (80 ml) dark rum
1 tsp ground cinnamon, or to taste
1 tsp ground cloves, or to taste
1 tsp ground allspice, or to taste
4 tbsp granulated sugar

IN THE MUG:
1 1/3 fl oz (40 ml) brandy
2 3/4 fl oz (80 ml) batter
warm milk
nutmeg

Separate the eggs in two bowls—one for yolks and one for whites. Whisk the egg whites until fluffy, and the yolks until creamy. Mix these together with rum and spices. Next, mix in the sugar and stir until you've got a smooth batter. Now you have the base.

Warm the cup with hot water before using it. In the cup, pour in the brandy, twice as much batter as brandy, and enough warm milk to fill the cup the rest of the way. Sprinkle nutmeg on top.

121

Inspiration
– classic drink books and examples

If you're ambitious when it comes to your profession, you're always searching for a chance to learn something new and to grow. When it comes to my profession, there is, of course, inspiration and ideas for flavor combinations to be found in the food and desserts served. Then there's travel, which is certainly the best way to hone your senses, and while abroad you'll get new impressions from everything you experience, but also from fellow bartenders you meet in their bars. With the Internet, many have begun to reach out to each other through Twitter and Facebook, and there are also plenty of cocktail fairs and expos around the world. Tales of the Cocktail in New Orleans distinguishes itself as the largest one, though the Manhattan Cocktail Classic and BCB (Bar Convent Berlin), to name a few, are also incredible. There, bartenders and other professionals meet to discuss new and old. There are seminars and parties for a few intense days, which is fun and stimulating, and you get the opportunity to meet bartenders from all over the world. And everyone knows that when you get to a city and want to have some good fun and see all the cool places, you've got to hang out with bartenders, which means that the next time you find yourself in another country and meet a sharp bartender at some convention, all you've got to do is find him again and you're guaranteed to have a great evening.

There are also some books that I couldn't get by without, and a few people to whom I owe a lot of thanks for my knowledge within this field. Some good friends, some inspirational bartenders, cocktail historians, and other authors. It's important for me to point out that I am not a cocktail historian; rather, I pulled the facts and dates in this book from other books, websites, and cocktail blogs that I read to satisfy my own thirst for knowledge. At the end of this book, I've put together a list for those who wish to delve deeper into the subject. I can emphatically recommend every single book, blog, and website on that list.

Recipes for Mixed Drinks

By Hugo R. Ensslin

SECOND EDITION

Occasionally, you get inspiration just from seeing what other bartenders have come up with. When Jim Meehan was visiting in Stockholm, he ran a pop-up bar where he interpreted Sweden in his cocktails. He made, for example, a minty drink that would have been very unusual to find in a Swedish bar. From there, we can also get some perspective on just how much we Swedes are influenced by classic American cocktails, and can try making our own interpretations of those.

A fizz is a drink with strong spirits, lemon, sugar, water (ice), and seltzer water, mentioned for the first time in Jerry Thomas's *The Bar-Tender's Guide* (1887). You can add egg whites to pretty much any fizz. I like the drink to be a bit rounder, so I almost always use egg whites. It also makes the drink look much nicer. I serve my fizzes in tall glasses without ice.

Gin Fizz

A proper classic. As mentioned, you can add egg whites in order to get a Silver Fizz. If you use an egg yolk instead, you get a Golden Fizz, and a whole egg gives you a Royal Fizz. Don't forget to dry-shake it if you add eggs (see page 10)!

2 1/3 fl oz (70 ml) gin
1 1/3 fl oz (40 ml) freshly squeezed
   lemon juice
1 fl oz (30 ml) simple syrup
1 2/3 fl oz (50 ml) seltzer water

Combine all the ingredients except the seltzer water in a shaker with ice; shake. Pour into a somewhat small highball glass and top with seltzer water. Finish off the drink by pressing the oil from a piece of lemon peel on top.

Morning Glory Fizz

Yet another so-called pick-me-up drink that was intended to be consumed in the morning after a night of drinking. It was in Harry Johnson's *New and Improved Bartender's Manual* (1888), and if you ask me, is one of the few truly good Scotch drinks.

When it comes to cocktails, I have a hard time working with the smokiness in Scotch. This is, of course, my own personal take on the matter, and there are plenty who love Scotch in drinks. I had even had enough of Scotch when the interest in single malt was reawakened some ten to fifteen years ago. Suddenly, every single guy with a suit wanted to stand up and tell all of his colleagues, and even us bartenders, about the deep wisdom he'd acquired from reading about the subject at the office. Or, worse yet, after having gone on a whisky-trip and bought their own barrel of it from some brewery in Scotland. I'm not kidding; at one time, you had to stand there every day and talk single malt with some know-it-all. Bartenders don't easily forget such things.

1 2/3 fl oz (50 ml) Scotch single malt
2/3 fl oz (20 ml) absinthe
2/3 fl oz (20 ml) fresh lemon juice
1 fl oz (30 ml) simple syrup
3/4 fl oz (25 ml) egg whites
1 2/3 fl oz (50 ml) seltzer water

Combine all the ingredients except for the seltzer water in a shaker. Dry-shake without ice, and then shake with ice. Pour into a smallish highball glass and top off with the seltzer water. Finish off the drink by pressing the oil of a piece of orange peel on top.

128

127

Ramos Gin Fizz (New Orleans Fizz)

A New Orleans classic invented by Henry C. Ramos in 1888; at the time, it went by the name of the New Orleans Fizz. I drank this one at the Sazerac Bar at the Roosevelt in New Orleans when I was last there, and learned that the Roosevelt has trademarked the name Ramos Gin Fizz. I don't know of any other trademarked drink . . .

The drink was and still is quite special, with orange blossom water, lemon, lime, and cream. It's not the most common combination and was probably one of the first drinks that didn't taste unbelievably strong due to the spirits, which at the time must have been absolutely fantastic. At the height of its popularity, there were thirty-four shaker boys at the Imperial Cabinet Saloon on Gravier Street, who would all be shaking the drink at the same time in order to keep up with demand. The thing with a Ramos, you see, is that it has to be shaken for twelve minutes!

ORANGE BLOSSOM WATER can usually be found at an asian grocery.

2 1/3 fl oz (70 ml) gin
2/3 fl oz (20 ml) fresh lemon juice
2/3 fl oz (20 ml) fresh lime juice
2/3 fl oz (20 ml) simple syrup
3/4 fl oz (25 ml) whipping cream
3/4 fl oz (25 ml) egg whites
3-4 splashes orange blossom water
1 1/3 fl oz (40 ml) seltzer water

This drink takes quite a bit of shaking! Combine all the ingredients except for the seltzer water in a shaker. Shake on ice for at least one minute; I recommend longer. Top off with the seltzer water and serve in a highball glass without ice. Finish it off by pressing out the oil from a piece of orange peel on top.

ramos gin fizz

Alabama Fizz

Sometimes, a drink can actually get too popular. There's just about nothing that bores a bartender more than spending the entire evening mixing the same drink. The Alabama Fizz is a good example of this. The drink is a Southside with seltzer water, and is also in *The Savoy Cocktail Book* from 1930. It's a real crowd-favorite when it's on a drink list. I've been forced to remove it from two different lists, because it would be the only thing we'd get to mix.

The combination of sweet, sour, and minty makes the Alabama Fizz the ultimate summer drink. Mint also appears to cause mass hysteria among bar patrons—once you've mixed a drink with mint, that's all anybody in the bar wants.

2 1/3 fl oz (70 ml) gin
a small handful of mint
1 fl oz (30 ml) simple syrup
1 1/3 fl oz (40 ml) freshly squeezed lemon juice
5 tsp (25 ml) egg whites
1 1/3 fl oz (40 ml) seltzer water

Vigorously shake the mint and syrup in a shaker. Add gin, lemon juice, and egg whites. Dry-shake without ice, and then shake with ice. Pour into a highball glass without ice and top off with seltzer water. Garnish with a sprig of mint.

Tom Collins

For me, a Collins is an easier variant of a fizz that I can build in a glass with ice instead of shaking it, and that doesn't contain egg whites.

This drink is said to have become popular in 1874, when "the great Tom Collins hoax" got started, which, if I understand correctly, was a joke that went like this:

Someone would ask: "Do you know Tom Collins?" upon which the one who was asked would respond that he did not. The asker would continue by telling him that Collins was at the nearest bar and had been talking about the one who was asked. This would cause the victim of the joke to rush to the nearest bar and inquire about a Tom Collins(?!) A sort of advertising campaign à la late 1800s, I suppose.

The drink was a success, and as proof of this, Jerry Thomas included it in *The Bar-Tender's Guide* from 1876.

2 1/3 fl oz (70 ml) gin
1 fl oz (30 ml) fresh lemon juice
2/3 fl oz (20 ml) simple syrup
1 2/3 fl oz (50 ml) seltzer water

Build on ice in a highball glass. Garnish with a piece of orange peel, which you press the oil out of, and a maraschino cherry.

132 Tom Collins

Create a new drink

There are probably as many ways to come up with a new drink as there are bartenders. But I'd wager to say that the majority of them work with one of the following methods: start with a drink that already exists, start with a good drink name, or start with a particular kind of spirit. No one way is better than any other; it all depends on what you want to end up with. Drinks created for different occasions, different drink lists, and different bars all require different approaches. What's most important, of course, is that the end result tastes good.

AMERICA, CLASSIC PARTY??
NEW CLASSIC, TWIST,
SOUR, FANCY

OR

When you make a new drink based on an existing one, it's common to start off with a classic. You can change the base alcohol, add new ingredients, or change the flavorings. In this way, you get a drink that feels like a classic, but with a twist.

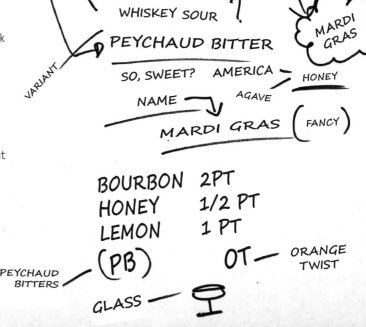

ANGOSTURA

BOURBON, NEW ORLEANS

WHISKEY SOUR ?

PEYCHAUD BITTER

VARIANT

SO, SWEET?   AMERICA

NAME   AGAVE

MARDI GRAS

MARDI GRAS (FANCY)

HONEY

BOURBON 2PT
HONEY   1/2 PT
LEMON   1 PT

(PB)   OT — ORANGE TWIST

PEYCHAUD
BITTERS

GLASS —

134

NAME! MO'HONEY MO'PROBLEMS

HONEY ∅ PROBLEM ☺

HONEY WATER — 1 PT HONEY , 1 PT WATER

A drink created for this book. I came up with the name and liked it, so I decided to make a bit of a challenge for myself. When I make new drinks, I most often start with bourbon, so I decided I wanted to use a different liquor. And tequila's one that a lot of people say they can't drink. Same goes for absinthe. Thus, I decided to use both, and balanced the sweetness from the absinthe and honey by pressing out the oil from a bit of lemon peel into the drink.

 FANCY

WHAT GOES WITH HONEY?
RUM, GIN, BOURBON, TEQUILA (EVERYTHING)

I LIKE BOURBON, BUT TEQUILA'S MORE OF A PROBLEM. ABSINTHE, TOO. SWEET, MAYBE? LEMON TWIST (LT), ABSINTHE SPRAY—COAT THE GLASS

 MO'HONEY MO'PROBLEMS.

TEQUILA (ARRETTE REPOSADO), HONEY, (LT) ABSINTHE SPRAY.

STIR TEQUILA, HONEY WATER ON ICE. SPRAY COCKTAIL GLASS W/ ABSINTHE (LT).

VODKA, CLASSIC, 🍸 —SHORT

KEEP THE FEEL OF THE LIQUOR

MOST CLASSIC—SCREWDRIVER

NEW VERSION—MODERN TWIST

STILL WITH ORANGE

I was given the challenge to create a new vodka-based cocktail. So, I took the world's simplest drink, vodka and orange juice, and made it somewhat more complicated while retaining the original flavor combination. And the name, then, became something of a play on the original.

ORANGE PEEL?   ORANGE BITTER?

CORDIAL — FLOWER ⟶ ORANGE FLOWER WATER

ORANGE CORDIAL ↓   ↑

VODKA, ORANGECORDIAL, OFW, OB

PLAY WITH THE NAME ↓

SCREWDRIVER ——— MONEY WRENCH

SWEDISH, WILD, LOCAL ← JOB
NOT TOO FANCY , APÉRITIF

SWEDISH - APPLE, BLACK CURRANTS, HONEY

FRENCH 75 SPIN —

 — TALL GLASS OR 🍸 COUPETTE

SWEETEN W/ HONEY —

WILD — BLACK CURRANT SCHNAPPS OR ELDERBERRY SCHNAPPS

BLACK CURRANTS, HONEY WATER, LEMON, TOP OFF WITH LOCAL APPLE CIDER OR MUST

When I was asked to make a welcome drink for a large party, I used a French 75 as my starting point—it being a perfect apéritif. We wanted to serve something wild, preferably with Swedish flavors. After a bit of consideration, I tested two very Swedish flavors: black currant and elderberry. The currants were the best, and instead of champagne, I decided on Swedish apple wine.

GARDEN COCKTAIL

Punch

Before juleps, cobblers, and Brandy Crustas, there was punch, or bål as we call it in Swedish. A punch is made of the following five basic ingredients: spirits, lemon, sugar, water, and spices. It's drunk in all social settings, and there are literary sources that show punch was consumed as early as the late 1600s. Even if it wasn't the first time alcohol had been mixed with fruit and spices, it was at least the first such drink to be globally recognized and appreciated. Personally, I think that punch is a splendid way of providing guests with a drink at a house party if you want to actually take part in the festivities yourself, rather than standing in the kitchen mixing drinks.

This book deals, of course, with cocktails and other drinks, so I'm not going to delve much farther into this subject, but I can strongly recommend *Punch: The Delights (and Dangers) of the Flowing Bowl* by Dave Wondrich. There is nobody who knows punch and cocktail history like old Dave. But still I feel like I ought to include a couple variants here. When it comes to punch, everything is in parts, since you can make as much or as little punch as you'd like.

GIN PUNCH

Gin Punch

A great sour variant with everyone's favorite combination of gin, lemon, and raspberry. You really can't go wrong with this one, and I've never heard of anybody who said they didn't like it. Gin Punch is a real crowd-pleaser, and if you make a pitcher of the same mixture, but with five parts water, leaving out the gin and champagne, you've got a perfect non-alcoholic thirst quencher, too. Your summer evening has been saved.

2 parts gin
1 part freshly squeezed lemon juice
2 parts water
1 part raspberry syrup (see page 13)
3 parts champagne

Combine all the ingredients; garnish with disc-shaped slices of orange and lemon. Top off with a few handfuls of fresh raspberries. You can toss in pretty much any fruit you want here, but I'm rather restrained when it comes to garnishes.

Jerry Thomas Manhattan

I've already written about this one as a cocktail, but this is the way it ought to be enjoyed. It's certainly a bit more of an advanced variant compared to Gin Punch, and you've got to appreciate strong spirits.

I'm quite taken with bitters and could increase the measurements to, say, 4 fl oz of each; naturally, some of it also has to do with what size parts you decide to use. Perhaps this sounds a bit corny, but making punch is a bit like making a stew, I'd say—you can taste it and steal some for yourself here and there as you go.

2 parts rye whiskey
1 part sweet vermouth
1/2 part Grand Marnier
2 fl oz (50 ml) Orange Bitters
2 fl oz (50 ml) Angostura Bitters
4 parts water

Mix all the ingredients together, and garnish with maraschino cherries and slices of orange.

Index